Nine Steps to Success

TEENS CAN MAKE IT HAPPEN

STEDMAN GRAHAM

A Fireside Book

Published by Simon & Schuster

New York London Toronto Sydney Singapore

FIRESIDE
Rockefeller Center
1230 Avenue of the Americas
New York, NY 10020

FIRESIDE and colophon are registered trademarks
of Simon & Schuster, Inc.

Designed by Ruth Lee

Manufactured in the United States of America

10   9   8   7   6   5   4   3   2   1

Library of Congress Cataloging-in-Publication Data
Graham, Stedman.
    Teens can make it happen : nine steps to success / Stedman Graham.
        p. cm.
    "A Fireside book."
    I. Success in adolescence. [I. Success.] I. title.

BF724.3.S9 G73 2000
158.1'0835—dc21   00-041271

ISBN 0-684-87082-7

Acknowledgments

Writing *You Can Make It Happen: A Nine-Step Plan for Success*—the predecessor to this book—has brought me great joy, and I am humbled by the response it continues to recieve. The people who stop me on the street, write letters, and attend my seminars consistently note the impact it has had on their lives.

I'm even more excited about *Teens Can Make It Happen*, a guide to teach young people the process for success, showing them how to find meaning in their lives. This book teaches practical concepts *and* how to apply them in the real world. My goal is to help young people understand as much as possible about how the world works so they can achieve all of their goals and aspirations, without limitations.

More than anything, *Teens Can Make It Happen* is about showing young people how to discover the hope and self-confidence they need to lead productive, healthy lives. This book is designed to help them develop lifestyles and processes that will prepare them for a lifetime of intellectual, emotional and physical awareness and well-being. Every chapter shows that you are not your *circumstances;* you are your *possibilities.*

I would especially like to thank a unique group of motivated, creative, open students at Shorewood High School in Shorewood, Wisconsin, who worked patiently, thoughtfully, and good-naturedly with us in adapting the nine steps for a young audience. These students serve as a lasting reminder that young people hold in their hands all the world's potential.

Thanks also to writer Tom Hanlon for his insightful contributions to this book, and to illustrator Christopher Evans for his imaginative drawings.

Finally, and as always, I am deeply grateful to my family, the people who motivate me to strive for success as a partner, father, son, uncle, cousin, and person throughout my life.

To all the youth
Who make it happen every day

Contents

1 The Success Process

Success is the result of perfection, hard work, learning from failure, loyalty and persistence.

Ret. U.S. Gen. Colin Powell

Let's begin with a tale of two teenagers.

Heather, seventeen, seems to be always in control, always confident. She has dreams and she pursues them. When she was in seventh grade, an acquaintance of her family became junior class president. Heather thought that was great, and she resolved to become a class president herself some day, which she did as a senior. Now she's considering which college to attend. She wants to be a physical therapist to help people.

11

Nick, sixteen, has always been interested in computers and has a great eye for design. He also has an entrepreneurial spirit—that is, he's always liked thinking of ways that he could put his talents to use and make money. In the past year he has spent his free time designing Web pages for various organizations and companies—at first, small organizations and companies within his town, and then larger corporations in other cities. In fact, he just agreed to design a Web site for a major retailer in the Midwest and will make $10,000 doing so. He wants to own his own multimedia business one day.

Heather and Nick are doing different things and have different career paths in front of them, but they have one important thing in common: They are following their dreams. They have visions for their lives, and they are not afraid to pursue those visions. Are you like Heather—confident, pursuing goals, going toward a bright future? Are you like Nick—using your strengths and abilities in ways that not only benefit you today but that can open up even greater possibilities for tomorrow?

Don't feel bad if you don't have a clear idea about what you want to do after you've graduated, or if you're not making $10,000 in your spare time. Many teenagers don't have a clear idea about what they want to do with their lives, and very few make that kind of money. In fact, the *money* that Nick is making through his entrepreneurial ideas is not the point. That's a result—and a very nice one— of his having a clear vision and not being afraid to follow it. *That's* the point—not only of Nick's story, but of this book. I want to help you create a vision for your life and a plan to make that vision happen.

I told you one thing that Heather and Nick have in common: their ability to pursue their dreams. Now I'll tell you one more thing they have in common. They don't worry about what others think about them or their plans. They're not spending time trying to impress others or wondering what other people think they should do. To spend time this way clouds your vision; you get too many conflicting thoughts, and ideas that don't match. If you can relate to that, you're not alone. In fact, for a long time I was right there with you.

Like many people, I wasted a great deal of my life worrying about what others thought of me. I still struggle with that, even though I now realize that it doesn't matter what others may think of me; what matters most is how I feel about myself, and that I believe in the *possibilities* for my life. When you have a sense of your own identity and a vision of where you want to go in your life, you can go after your dreams for a fulfilling life. And that's what this book is all about.

In this chapter we'll begin to explore what it means to live a successful life. We'll help you understand:

- What it means to develop a vision and act on that vision;
- How you can use a tool called "Success Circles" to help you focus on a fulfilling life; and
- How to begin taking the nine steps toward living that successful life.

The average person generally develops only about two percent of his or her potential. That leaves plenty of room for bettering yourself! In order to do so, though, you need vision. You can't go anywhere if you can't see where you're going.

Developing a Vision

Vision, simply stated, is seeing your purpose in life. It's tied in to knowing who you are and what you can *envision* yourself doing with your talents and desires. We all have talents and we all have desires. What we need to learn is how to use those talents and desires in living fulfilling lives. Opportunities are there for all of us, but we have to seize the right ones for us based on our own visions for our lives.

Creating a vision and making that vision happen take what I call an "active optimism": You have to believe in yourself and in your future, and then you have to actively pursue your plans. Most teenagers have great optimism for the future. The *1999–2000 State of Our Nation's Youth* report by the Horatio Alger Association of Distinguished Americans gave voice to teens across our nation on a variety of issues. Based on that report, about seven out of ten teens believe two things about opportunities:

1. The harder they work, the more opportunities will be available to them.
2. They will have many opportunities available to them after they graduate from high school.

Hopefully you're one of those seven in ten who see many opportunities before you. It's hard to develop a vision for bettering your life if you don't believe you have many opportunities for doing so.

We can't all be professional athletes or movie stars, of course. And we can't all get the lead in the school play, be class president, be the star on the basketball team, or be in the National Honor Society. But we all have the ability to lead dynamic lives by pursuing our own unique goals and dreams. The poorest, the weakest, or the least popular of us has the power within to pursue a fulfilling life. We must believe that it is possible to achieve our dreams and then commit to achieving those dreams. Without that belief, every dream will turn to dust.

Do you believe that you can take control of your own life? Are you pursuing goals? Are you trying to better yourself, to learn, to grow, to make good choices?

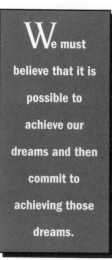

W**e must believe that it is possible to achieve our dreams and then commit to achieving those dreams.**

Heather is confident about who she is, about her value, and she focuses on her goals. She is actively controlling her own life, driven by her goals and principles. People like Heather understand that what happens to them is not nearly as important as how they choose to respond to it. People like Nick see how they can use their talents and are not afraid to take risks. They see the positive side of taking risks and see potential in a variety of opportunities.

It's not easy to change your life. You need to build strong and supportive relationships as you follow the Success Process. Take control and focus on pursuing a good life, but don't isolate yourself in the process. Isolating yourself is not healthy spiritually, mentally, or physically, and it certainly is not the way to achieve your dreams. Nobody makes it alone. You need friends—friends who believe in you.

As you follow the steps in this book, build solid relationships and lean on them when you need to. Don't be afraid to ask for help or encouragement along the way. And look to provide that helping hand or word of encouragement to others, too.

Success Circles

You can't do much about what others may say or think about you. You can only focus on those things that are within your control. The things that matter most to you and that you have the power to influence are inside what I call your "Success Circles."

Anyone could come up with a dozen or more such circles, but let's consider these basic three: *Career, Personal Development,* and *Relationships.*

- By "Career" we mean the things you can do now to help yourself to the type of career you envision for yourself.
- "Personal Development" refers to how you want to develop as a person. Your development will affect not only you, but the community around you, as you see opportunities to give back to your community.

- Finally, "Relationships" are critical at every stage of our lives; no person is successful in isolation.
- Through these three areas you can begin to create an enjoyable life for yourself and generate success both now and for your future.

On a sheet of paper, draw three Success Circles, one for each category listed. Within each one, try to list at least five things you can do to better your life. For instance, your Circles might begin to shape up like this:

Career

- Be more consistent with homework.
- Hook up with a study partner.
- Get a summer job in the type of business that interests me (e.g., be an aide in a hospital if you're interested in a medical field).
- Take more advanced courses in my area of career interest.
- Take a variety of courses to expand my career opportunities.
- Talk with and learn from people who are working in my area of career interest.

Personal Development

- Work through my Success Club to better know myself, my needs, and my desires.
- Define what success and achievement mean for me.
- Start jogging or working out regularly.
- Volunteer at summer camp.
- Take part in a walk-a-thon.

Relationships

- Get along better with my parents.
- Be more open in talking about things that are really bothering me.
- Be supportive and encouraging to my close friends.
- Get to know someone in my field of interest who can begin to "show me the ropes" (e.g., if you want to be a coach, choose a coach you want to model yourself after and strike up a relationship so you can begin to learn from that coach).
- Help my grandparents with house and yard work.

If things aren't going well for you in one of these areas, chances are it has a negative impact on the other areas. That's why it is so important to have a balanced life, paying attention to your schoolwork; your job if you have one; your per-

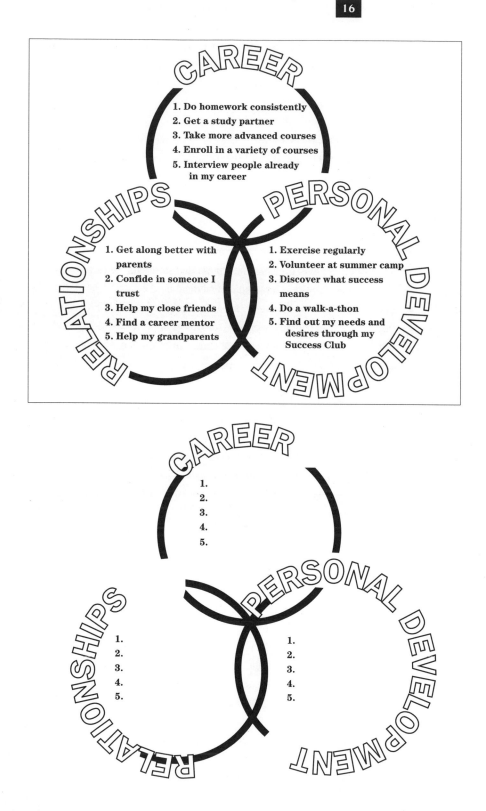

CAREER

1. Do homework consistently
2. Get a study partner
3. Take more advanced courses
4. Enroll in a variety of courses
5. Interview people already in my career

RELATIONSHIPS

1. Get along better with parents
2. Confide in someone I trust
3. Help my close friends
4. Find a career mentor
5. Help my grandparents

PERSONAL DEVELOPMENT

1. Exercise regularly
2. Volunteer at summer camp
3. Discover what success means
4. Do a walk-a-thon
5. Find out my needs and desires through my Success Club

CAREER

1.
2.
3.
4.
5.

RELATIONSHIPS

1.
2.
3.
4.
5.

PERSONAL DEVELOPMENT

1.
2.
3.
4.
5.

sonal development and the community around you; and your relationships with family, friends, and adults who are in positions to help you.

Also, please note that often your circles will overlap. For example:

- Through an advanced class you're taking in your field of interest, a teacher might introduce you to someone in that field who could act as a mentor or guide.
- You might develop a key relationship while volunteering at a summer camp.
- Through an important relationship your eyes might be opened to an exciting career opportunity.

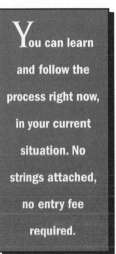

You can learn and follow the process right now, in your current situation. No strings attached, no entry fee required.

This overlapping strengthens your life in these key areas and gives you a more solid base from which to pursue a successful life.

The circles are simply a way of helping you focus on the most important areas of your life when you undertake the Success Process. That focus helps you to grow and enrich your life.

Now I'm going to tell you a secret about this process for pursuing success: *It's not complicated.* The Success Process has been around for thousands of years. People from all walks of life have followed it and lived it. It doesn't depend on your bloodlines. It's not an exclusive club that only the rich can buy into. You don't have to be a genius or a budding Pulitzer Prize winner to learn the process. *You can learn and follow the process right now, in your current situation. No strings attached, no entry fee required. Step up to the plate. Success is awaiting you, if you want it. Do you want it?*

Steps to a Better Life

Take a look around you. The Success Process is being lived out by people ranging from athletes to civil rights and civic leaders, to business giants, to teachers and parents, to students.

When most people think of successful students, they think of the high achievers in the classroom, on the playing fields and courts, and in music and the arts. Indeed, these are all important areas of growth and learning and success. But how about teenagers in the world of business, teenagers as entrepreneurs? Teens are finding success here, too. In fact, the Bureau of Labor lists more than 87,000 *self-employed* sixteen- to nineteen-year-olds. Like Nick, many teens are

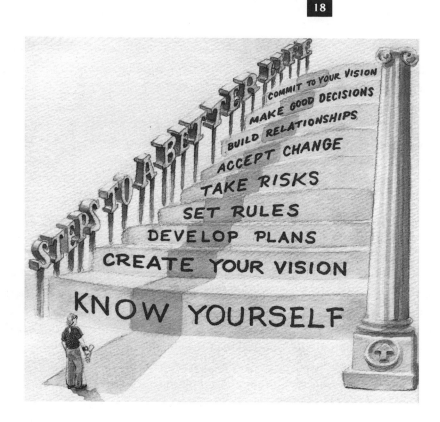

finding they don't have to wait to become an adult before they taste success in business. Here are just a few of their success stories:

- A seventeen-year-old basketball player is in his fifth year of running a two-week basketball camp for kids. The camp started with fifteen kids participating; it now has 70. The camp has brought in more than $2,500 in each of the last two summers for the player.
- An eighteen-year-old who began mowing lawns in sixth grade now has his own landscaping service, complete with trucks, equipment, and employees. His company provides lawn services for ninety-one houses per week.
- A fourteen-year-old runs his own desktop publishing business, creating letterheads and business cards for clients.
- Two 1999 high school graduates build Web sites for various clients, charging $50 to $60 per hour for Web site development and earning from $1,500 to $7,000 per client. They are using part of the money toward their college education and investing the rest.

The list could go on and on. Perhaps reading these success stories will spark you to add your own to the list. "The key is to dream," says one of the teenage entrepreneurs, "to think what's possible and then have the passion to do it."

Begin with the dream. Then pursue it with passion. If you can dream, and if you can pursue things with passion, you are well on your way. From your dream you will begin to shape your vision, and from your vision you will make a plan to pursue that vision, to make that dream come true. But you need the passion to follow through.

And don't be afraid to dream. Some people scoff at dreaming, maybe because they're afraid to risk it themselves. They'd rather stay in the hole they're in than pursue a way out. Successful people don't think that way.

I mentioned earlier that you don't have to be rich or smart or have royalty in your bloodlines to be successful. Another great thing about this Success Process is that you can begin it anywhere, anytime. Remember Heather and Nick? They seem well on their way to success; they have their routes planned and their bags packed, so to speak.

Your route may not be as well planned as Heather's or Nick's, but you have just as much opportunity for success as they do. You may be in a tough situation and may not immediately see a clear path to a bright future, but you still have options and choices to make that can help you be successful in life. You still have opportunities ahead of you.

So what are the nine steps to success that I've referred to? Here is a brief summary of my Nine-Step Plan for Success. Each step is a chapter.

Step 1: Check Your ID

Before you can decide what you want for your life, you must first understand who you are, what the influences are in your life, why you act and think the way you do. Some describe this as searching for *self-awareness*. I call it *checking your ID*. Before you take off on any serious journey these days, you must first make sure that you have valid identification with you. The same holds true for your journey on the Success Process.

Step 2: Create Your Vision

To seek a better life, you have to decide what you want for your life. What are your dreams and aspirations? What characteristics, talents, and skills do you bring to the table? I'll help you explore these areas and then set ambitious but realistic goals.

Step 3: Develop Your Travel Plan

Once you have established your goals, you need a plan to pursue your vision. In this step, I will help you develop that plan. I will also show you how to chart the best path by using your values as your markers.

Step 4: Master the Rules of the Road

Every day you will encounter distractions that might stop you or slow you down in your journey. In this step, I will teach you how to "keep on keeping on." I will provide keys to self-motivation so that you will have the strength not to be easily distracted or defeated.

Step 5: Step into the Outer Limits

There are always risks when you pursue a dream. To grow, you have to leave your comfort zone and enter unknown territory. But without taking those risks and facing your fears, you'll never get to where you want to be. You may fail sometimes, but you will never succeed if you are not willing to risk failure. And even if you do fail, you can learn from the experience and try again. To do that, you will need courage, and you will also need to have faith in your ability to achieve your goals.

Step 6: Pilot the Seasons of Change

Many people never go after their dreams for a better life because they are afraid of change, afraid they will lose something that has been important to them. But think about this: It is impossible to move ahead while staying where you are. You have to be willing to accept that some changes will be necessary. Many people keep doing the same thing over and over again in their lives, hoping that something better will come along. But if you keep doing what you have always done, you will get the same results. If you are not getting what you want out of life, you have to change your approach to it. Ride out the tough times and be patient for the changes you want to become real. Give yourself time to accept changes and adjust to them.

Step 7: Build Your Dream Team

Supportive relationships that help you work toward your goals are critical to your success. To build those relationships, you need to learn to trust others. And to earn their trust, you in turn must be trustworthy.

Step 8: Win by a Decision

Making decisions wisely is one of your greatest challenges. This involves assessing your personal strengths, needs, and resources; checking them against your beliefs and values; and making decisions based on that assessment. You need a strong heart and a wise mind to do that.

Step 9: Commit to Your Vision

In this step, I will review all of the previous material with you and then teach you how to make a true commitment to achieving your vision for a successful life. You can set all the goals and make all the plans in the world, but unless you truly commit yourself to going after them, you'll never achieve them. You have to pursue your vision with energy and make that pursuit a priority in your life.

Those are the nine steps to success. They're not a mystery, and they're not a miracle cure. They're tools for you to use to build value in your life.

Now let's take the first step: checking your ID.

2 Check Your ID

Who I am is what fulfills me and fulfills the vision I have of the world.

Audre Lorde

In the last chapter we talked about the importance of believing in *possibilities.* It's unlikely that you'll lead a successful life if you don't believe you have many possibilities. But you need more than that belief: You need to know who you are.

I'm not talking about your name, your phone number, your social security number, your driver's license. I'm not talking about your grade-point average, your I.Q., or how many brothers and sisters you have. I'm not talking about what your parents do or don't do. I'm talking about *you:* what makes you tick, what drives you, what interests you, what you excel in or would like to excel in. I'm talking about the dreams you have for yourself, which may not necessarily be the dreams others may have for you.

I'm talking about the *real you*. Chances are, you haven't fully discovered the real you yet. You may have some clues, or you may be—at least at this moment—clueless. But until you are clued in, until you know who you really are, you won't be able to give shape and focus to those possibilities that exist in your life.

When you begin to focus on *your* possibilities, based on who *you* are, then those possibilities evolve from a generic "it's out there for everyone" idea to something that begins to be molded specifically by *your* personality, *your* strengths and dreams, *your* traits. In essence, you use this self-understanding, this self-awareness, to shape your vision for your life.

Let me tell you a little story about self-awareness. But first I must mention that for the last twelve years I have been involved in a relationship with one of the most extraordinary and famous women in the world. You may feel as if you know me because of my relationship with Oprah Winfrey. If that relationship is your *only* measure of me, you really don't know me at all, of course. None of us are defined simply by our relationships, nor are we defined by how people perceive us. It is up to each one of us to define ourselves, and that is a life's work.

Not too long ago, I was walking on Michigan Avenue in Chicago when a construction worker, crossing the street with me, said, "Hey, Oprah's boyfriend, how's it going?"

There was a time when I might have ignored the guy or given him a cold stare for calling me that. But instead, I reached out, shook his hand, and began talking with him. We walked across the street together and continued our conversation on the street corner. By the end of the conversation, he wasn't calling me "Oprah's boyfriend" anymore. He was calling me "Mr. Graham."

That construction worker had no idea how long it took me to learn to handle situations like that gracefully. For a long time, it bothered me when people treated me as nothing more than *Oprah's boyfriend*. But as I developed the Success Process that is the heart of this book, I learned how to deal with people who don't really know me; I also learned to know myself.

Do you know yourself? Life can be tough when you feel all the time that you have to prove yourself, that you're a victim of mistaken identity. Self-knowledge and self-understanding are essential to pursuing a better life. In this chapter we'll explore:

- Knowing who you are, knowing why you respond to certain people and situations in certain ways;
- Using self-understanding as the cornerstone to building a successful life;
- Overcoming obstacles and going through the sometimes painful process of shedding your protective shell;

- Replacing negative thoughts with positive thoughts; and
- Rescripting your life through the three Cs: confidence, competence, and capability.

Let's begin with the most essential item: knowing who you are.

Validating Your ID: Knowing Who You Are

You can't open a bank account, drive a car, or even get into a gym to attend a high school game without showing valid identification. And you can't reach your full potential unless you also first validate your identity by knowing exactly who you are and where you want to go.

You have an invalid ID when you don't understand yourself and your actions. *Why did I get so upset when my parents didn't allow me to go to that party? Why am I so nervous around this boy or that girl?* You validate your identity when you come to understand yourself. You do that by realizing what motivates you and flips your emotional switches. When somebody says or does something to you that makes you moody or angry, it might not affect your best friend's mood at all, even though the friend cares about you and how you feel. You're doing all you can to keep from flying off the handle while your friend is hanging there, totally at ease with the situation. And you stand there amazed that your friend can have such a reaction. For instance:

> I said she had no right to talk to me like that—who did she think she was, my mother? Then she said something nasty about my mother, and that did it. My mother has worked two jobs for the last seven years so we could have enough food on the table to eat. I tell you, I wanted to get it on right then and there. But my friend Cassie says, "Why do you care what she says? Why even waste your time listening to her?" She got me to chill out. But it wasn't easy. That girl got me going, let me tell you. I don't even know why, but she did.
>
> Yolanda, age 18

Once you understand where those emotions and attitudes come from, then you can begin to understand not only why you act the way you do, but also why others see you the way they do. This understanding gives you the power to change and control your behavior in a more positive and effective manner. It allows you to begin acting on the steps you put into each of your Success Circles.

The first step in understanding who you are is to examine the things that influence your behavior. You'll do that in the following worksheet. This can be painful; it can mean confronting some serious issues and realities in your life. The poet and author Maya Angelou, who has not had an easy life, once said, "Success is not fame or fortune. It is picking up that burden and keeping on walking and not letting the pain trip you up."

■ Reality Check: Who Are You?

Describe your five best features or characteristics: What do you like about yourself? Are you hardworking? Kind? Thoughtful? Serious? Fun-loving? Honest? Reliable? Realize that sometimes your *best* features may be hidden; they may not be your most obvious features. Choose the ones that describe you at your *best:*

1. I am _____

2. I am _____

3. I am _____

4. I am _____

5. I am _____

Who are the type of people you most admire? Why?

_____

_____

_____

If you could be like anyone, who would it be? Why?

_____

_____

_____

What makes you happy?

_____

_____

_____

What makes you sad?

_____

_____

_____

What are the three things you are most afraid of, and why?

1. _____

2. _____

3. _____

How have your fears influenced any decisions in your life?

_____

_____

_____

_____

_____

What are three characteristics that may be holding you back from being more successful in your life?

1. _____

2. _____

3. _____

What experiences have caused you to develop these characteristics?

_____

_____

_____

_____

_____

What has been the biggest challenge in your life so far?

_____

_____

_____

_____

_____

When you are faced with a challenge, what is your typical reaction?

_____

_____

_____

_____

_____

Take a look one year down the road. What kind of person do you see yourself being? Imagine that you see yourself walking down a hallway. Describe yourself—not just in physical terms, but in terms of the features and talents that are beginning to shine.

_____

_____

_____

_____

_____

Building Success through Self-Understanding

To know yourself is the first, and most important, step in the process of pursuing your dreams and goals. You need to become secure enough in who you are to accept the influence of others on you. If you aren't secure in yourself, odds are you won't be open to the love, constructive criticism, and suggestions of those around you.

27

I discovered this when I began searching to find out why Oprah's fame and the public response to our relationship was so crippling for me. When I went inward and found the cause of that hurt, I learned a great deal about myself. I began to understand and accept myself to the degree that I became free to create a vision for my life, a better life than I might ever have designed if I hadn't been

forced to really look at the influences, good and bad, that determined my actions and my feelings.

That journey, in part, is what inspired me to write this book, so that others, too, might find their own way. Although people tell me that I appear to be a self-confident person, the truth is that, like many people, I have struggled with insecurity for a great deal of my life. My lack of self-confidence traces back to my youth and my family's circumstances.

I'll never forget what happened to me one day in Mister T.A.'s, a small coffee shop where teenagers hung out in my hometown of Whitesboro, New Jersey. It was owned by T. A. Richardson. I was bragging to him about all of the college scholarship offers I was getting—I had earned All-State honors in basketball—and he looked up at me and said, "You'll never go to college because your family is too stupid." He was referring to my two youngest brothers, Jimmy and Darry, who are developmentally disabled. There had been a great deal of shame cast upon my family because of my brothers and their disabilities.

To know yourself is the first, and most important, step in the process of pursuing your dreams and goals.

Oh, that hurt. I tried so hard to prove myself to people in the town, but there always seemed to be someone ready to shoot me down with a reference to my brothers and their disabilities. The jabs and put-downs caused me to put even more pressure on myself. I participated in nearly every school activity I could get into. I was a drum major and a class leader and an athlete. And yet, back then it seemed like nothing I accomplished could erase that stigma.

Four years later, after completing college, I was back in Whitesboro and I stopped by T. A. Richardson's place. I was wary of him still, but he surprised me by greeting me warmly and telling me how proud he was that I'd gotten my degree. I didn't remind him of what he had said to me. He had probably forgotten it, but I certainly hadn't. Now I wonder if he had said that cruel thing to me in order to motivate me. It was painful and is still painful to recall, but his words certainly did motivate me. In times when school wasn't going well, I'd think about what T.A. had said, and then I'd get back to work.

As a child, I felt I was alone in my insecurities, and I felt I had to make it alone. I know now that we all have problems. We all have obstacles to overcome. I have also come to understand that there are many people willing to accept and help you, if only you first accept and help yourself. It's true. If you are an angry person, the hostility drives people away from you, but if you are at peace and have confidence in yourself, people are drawn to you.

> I used to get in a lot of fights, a lot of trouble. I don't so much anymore, but now I got this rap. People say, "Oh, there goes Robert, don't mess with him, he'll do you bad," but that ain't true. That ain't me anymore. But most folks stay away from me 'cause they're afraid of me.
>
> Robert, age 17

People stay away from Robert because they feel that he's an angry person. Robert has a very real obstacle to overcome.

Overcoming Obstacles

We all have obstacles to overcome. As I've just described, one of mine was the stigma attached to my brothers' disabilities and the resulting low expectations others had for me. Another was being taunted in school as "Whitey" because of my light skin color. Among blacks I felt I had to prove I was as black as anyone else; among whites I felt I had to prove my worth even more.

Obstacles come in all shapes and sizes. Racism. Sexism. Elitism. You want to be a star athlete, maybe one day a professional athlete, but your athletic abilities are only average. (Adults who knowingly mislead young people in this regard—telling them "You could be a star!"—aren't much better than guys selling drugs to kids on street corners. Both are peddling false dreams.) You want to be taken seriously, for your thoughts and opinions to be valued; but you have the reputation of someone who's always joking around and thus no one listens to you.

Part of knowing who you are, then, is understanding the obstacles you face, and understanding how to get around those obstacles so that your gifts and abilities can flourish. It's quite common to put a protective shell around yourself when you face a serious obstacle. You try to hide what you or others perceive as a shortcoming or a flaw. But that's not *overcoming* an obstacle; that's avoiding it— and in doing so, allowing it to negatively impact your life. Don't shrink back from your obstacle, but face it and consider it in a new light. You need to change your way of thinking.

Thinking Positively

To be successful, you should feel free to go after what you want in life. How do you do that? You become a positive, energized person. You don't think poorly of yourself or have a negative attitude. You get rid of negative baggage that holds you back. You believe in yourself, and in doing so you give others cause to believe in you, too.

In the last chapter I defined vision as seeing your purpose in life, envisioning who you are and what you're about and how you spend your time and energy. It's also about how you pursue your dreams and how you use your talents and abilities in that pursuit.

When your vision focuses on your potential and the possibilities rather than on your past and your limitations, then you can be helped by others and help them in return. Sometimes you first have to get a grip on the feelings and beliefs that have held you back and limited your sense of who you are before you can move forward.

"You're stupid. What do you know?"

"Don't put her in the game! She can't play!"

"Who would want to go out with you?"

"What a nerd!"

Have any of these types of comments been directed your way? It's easy to start believing the message even if it isn't true. To think positively, you first have to identify the negative messages that make you feel bad or incapable and replace them with more positive thoughts. For instance, instead of thinking, *That guy was being disrespectful of me; he was telling me I'm nothing more than Oprah's boyfriend,* I learned to change my thinking: *This guy doesn't know me except through Oprah's fame. He is just excited at seeing someone he considers a celebrity, and he said the first thing that came out of his mouth. I can handle it.*

When you think more positively, you become more confident. This in turn helps you to feel more competent and capable. You see your negative thoughts in a different light: *Hey, I'm not stupid! Jasmine's just ticked off about something.* You realize that you used to automatically agree with whatever others would say about you, whether positive or negative. The negative thoughts were not only painful; many of them were wrong. Believing negative and false statements about you is like putting shackles on your legs and then wondering why you can't run.

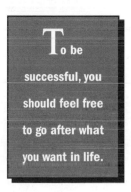

To be successful, you should feel free to go after what you want in life.

Consider the positive aspects of your life; this adds to your sense of self-worth. Consider your personality, your talents and gifts, or something or someone of value in your personal history or background. I remember picking up a book in my hometown library one day and finding an account of the life of my great-uncle, former U.S. Congressman George H. White. It was so inspiring and it gave me a sense of history and value to know that he was part of my family. He was a lawyer who practiced in Washington, D.C., and Philadelphia, and a major landowner and developer along the Jersey shore. In Congress in the late 1800s, he created legislation and lobbied for fairness, equality, and justice.

U.S. Representative White introduced the first antilynching legislation on the federal level. In his farewell to his fellow congressmen, who had not welcomed him because he was a black man, he called upon them to "Obliterate race hatred, party prejudice, and help us to achieve nobler ends, greater results, and become satisfactory citizens."

So in addition to considering your own positive aspects, focus on the high achievers in your family and celebrate their lives rather than dwelling on negative images. Take time to consider what may be holding you back as well as what can be positive influences.

■ Turning Obstacles into Opportunities

What has been the most negative influence on your life?

_____

_____

_____

How has that negative influence affected how you perceive yourself and how you behave?

_____

_____

_____

Part of being successful is turning negative influences into learning experiences and opportunities for growth. Have you been able to do this? If so, how? If not, how do you think some people are able to turn a negative into a positive?

_____

_____

_____

Name any obstacles that keep you from being the "real you," or that keep you from doing what you want to do or being what you want to be.

_____

_____

_____

What are ways around your obstacles? Don't fall into the trap of thinking there *is* no way around them. It may take the help of other people, but there is *always* a way around—or through, or under, or over—any obstacle.

_____

_____

_____

What areas of your life are most difficult to share with others? Are there areas or issues that you're protective of? Why?

_____

_____

_____

If you were more vulnerable to family and close friends, if you were able to talk about some of these difficult issues or concerns, what do you think would happen?

_____

_____

_____

How can opening up and coming out of your protective shell help you on your road to living a more successful life?

_____

_____

_____

Successful people are always creating opportunities for themselves to continue to grow, learn, and be successful. Think of the three Success Circles—Career, Personal Development, and Relationships—or other important areas of success for you. How can you create opportunities for growth and greater success in those areas?

1. In my Career Circle I can . . .

_____

_____

_____

2. In my Personal Development Circle I can . . .

_____

_____

_____

3. In my Relationships Circle I can . . .

_____

_____

_____

4. In other important Success Circles I can . . .

_____

_____

_____

Using The Three *C*s in Rescripting Your Life

I'm not suggesting that achieving success is easy. It is not. But if you can understand who you are and where you want to go, if you can believe in the possibilities for your life, and if you feel like you deserve your dreams and goals, you are well on your way in the process.

I believe that to be successful you must have the "three *C*s": confidence, competence, and capability.

Confidence. You must believe in yourself and feel worthy of your vision. You have to feel that you deserve success:

- "I should be a starter on the softball team. I'm a good hitter and a great fielder."
- "I'm going to ace my chemistry test because I've done the work. I'm prepared and I know the content."
- "I'm going to get that summer internship at the newspaper. I'm mature and have the skills they're looking for. I've got good clips to show them from the school newspaper."

You gain confidence by concentrating on your talents and accomplishments and personal history that make you special and unique.

Competence. We are all competent in different areas. You may be great in math and science but dread English class; one of your friends may love literature and excel in writing or drama but break into a cold sweat at the prospect of taking the easiest biology class. This example refers to a specific competence that you can fairly easily measure by how well you do at whatever the task or project is. As you become more competent at a variety of things, you begin to build not only skills, but an attitude that you, at your core, are a competent person. This is an invaluable attitude to have in your pursuit of success.

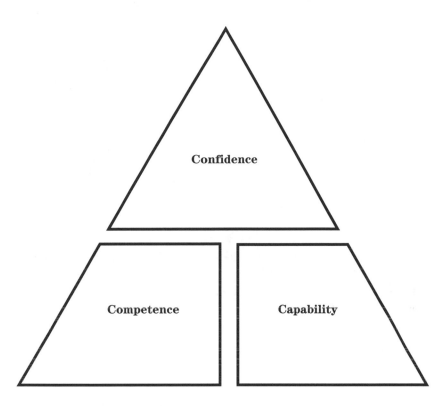

Capability. Capability is about a "can-do" attitude. It's one that is charged with energy, because you know you can do something. You must feel capable of defining, creating, and controlling your own life. Start small with something such as going out for an extracurricular activity or becoming certified as a lifeguard or working out for thirty minutes a day. Do it, and then challenge yourself to do something else, such as taking a painting class or writing in your journal every day. After you attain small goals, you can work up to bigger ones, proving to yourself and others that you have the power to control your life—that you are capable.

Chances are you'll feel confident, competent, and capable if you have a strong support system around you. For many of us that support begins with our family, but it can also come from others—friends, teachers, coaches, guidance counselors, ministers or rabbis. Such a support system helps you feel good about yourself and focus on your strengths and gifts. People with positive self-images believe in themselves and in their abilities to control their own lives.

On the other hand, if you have low self-esteem, you'll have to work at getting those "three Cs" going in your life. There are many causes of low self-esteem. If you are constantly criticized and deprived of praise you might come to accept that inferior image of yourself. You might believe that you do not have the power to do anything about your life. If you feel that you have little or no value, chances are you do not feel worthy of success. Perhaps you do not feel as though you deserve to have your deepest needs and desires recognized or realized. Your vision becomes severely limited, and your life a self-fulfilling prophecy. You live down to low expectations rather than up to high expectations.

For example, let's say your parents have always praised your older brother's academic achievements; they have high expectations for him to do well in school. Your brother *does* do well in school and, fueled by your parents' praise and their expectations, he finds himself at the top of his class with straight As. His ability, coupled with the praise and high expectations, translate into academic success for him.

But for some reason, your parents have never shown you the same interest or given you the praise you've deserved for your own academic achievements. In fact, compared to how they treat your brother, they all but ignore your schoolwork and achievements. It's obvious they don't expect you to do as well. You begin to think that maybe your brother got all the brains in the family. You hope to squeeze by in school. You do as little as possible to get by, and you do what you can to draw little attention to yourself. Ds would make your parents upset, so you get mainly Cs with a few Bs sprinkled in.

> Chances are you'll feel confident, competent, and capable if you have a strong support system around you.

You are meeting their expectations of mediocrity. That's what a self-fulfilling prophecy is: You begin to believe the negative messages that others feed you until you have low expectations for yourself, and you fulfill those low expectations, even though you may be able to do much better. Who knows? You may be just as gifted academically as your brother. But as long as you listen to the message you are receiving from your parents, you'll never know.

All the way through grade school I was told I was stupid. Teachers didn't spend any time with me because I was considered a waste of time, I guess. No one expected anything of me—except my grandfather. He took me aside one time in eighth grade after I'd gotten in trouble. I'd been in a few fights and gotten mainly D's on my report card. He put his hand on my shoulder and said, "James, why are you doing this? What's going on?" I shrugged my shoulders; I certainly didn't know what was going on and didn't much care. He gave me an understanding smile. His eyes pierced into me, but they were warm and compassionate and understanding. And I saw something else in there, too: I saw that he believed in me.

He said, "I see you doing great things as you grow up. You've got some special gifts, and when you open up to them, the whole world is going to open up for you. And all this will be a million miles away." At first I didn't know what to think, but I saw how much he believed in me. It wasn't just a line he was feeding me. He saw something in me that no one else had—or at least that no one else had bothered to tell me.

That day I began to change the way I thought about myself. I'm certain that without my grandfather, my troubled childhood would have turned very naturally into a troubled life as an adult.

James, age 24, medical student

You have to have someone you trust and believe in help you see how competent and capable you are and tell you the truth. Armed with this truth, you can step back and begin to see yourself and your life with a clear vision.

You need to stop believing the lies that others have told you about yourself and start to believe in the possibilities for your life. You can, in essence, *rescript* your life, focusing on the areas you're competent and capable in. If your life is in a rut, if you do things that ultimately drag you down, then chances are you're listening to the wrong people, to the people who don't see your strengths. Chances are you have this little voice inside you saying, *I'm no good. I don't deserve anything. I'm nothing special.*

If you listen to those thoughts, it doesn't matter how competent and capable you are; you'll stay stuck and will be an *underachiever.* You won't achieve nearly what you could, based on your gifts and talents.

So what do you do if you hear thoughts like that inside your own head? Stop the thoughts. Pretend they're on a tape recorder. See yourself hitting the "stop" button. Then rewind to the beginning of the tape and record a *new* message, one that's positive, that focuses on your strengths, your abilities, and what makes you special.

We've talked about the importance of confidence, competence, and capability. Now it's your turn. In the next worksheet we'll help you focus on a positive self-image by highlighting your talents and achievements. Tell us what you've done that shows your confidence, competence, and capability.

37

■ Noting Your Talents and Achievements

When are you most confident? Why? List five situations or areas in which you feel confident.

1. I am confident in (or when) . . .

_____

_____

_____

2. I am confident in (or when) . . .

_____

_____

_____

3. I am confident in (or when) . . .

_____

_____

_____

4. I am confident in (or when) . . .

_____

_____

_____

5. I am confident in (or when) . . .

_____

_____

_____

List five areas that you feel competent in, based on your experience. It could be in broad areas such as academics, sports, or music, or it could be in skills or situations, such as being a loyal friend, a good listener, an encourager; being understanding; and so on.

1. I am competent in (or at) . . .

_____

_____

_____

2. I am competent in (or at) . . .

_____

_____

_____

3. I am competent in (or at) . . .

_____

_____

_____

4. I am competent in (or at) . . .

_____

_____

_____

5. I am competent in (or at) . . .

_____

_____

_____

What are your capabilities? List five things you are capable of being or doing.

1. I am capable of (or at) . . .

_____

_____

_____

2. I am capable of (or at) . . .

_____

_____

_____

3. I am capable of (or at) . . .

_____

_____

_____

4. I am capable of (or at) . . .

_____

_____

_____

5. I am capable of (or at) . . .

_____

_____

_____

What are some of your proudest achievements?

_____

_____

_____

_____

_____

Why did they make you proud?

_____

_____

_____

_____

_____

Based on your achievements, what do you think you are capable of doing in the next two to five years?

_____

_____

_____

TEENS CAN MAKE IT HAPPEN

_____

_____

_____

In thinking of your competencies or talents, which ones give you the greatest pleasure?

_____

_____

_____

_____

_____

_____

Which ones do you think you'd like to continue to use and develop during the next five years?

_____

_____

_____

_____

_____

_____

When you're not feeling confident or competent or capable, what are things you might do, or thoughts you might have, that can help you turn a negative into a positive?

_____

_____

41

_____

_____

_____

Share your worksheet responses with someone who is perceptive, who knows you well, and who will give you honest opinions. Ask this person if he or she agrees with what you've written, or if he or she can see other strengths in you as well. You may be surprised; sometimes those who know you well can identify talents and gifts in you that you're not aware of.

If you had trouble filling out the worksheet, don't feel bad. It's more a result of your not knowing yourself well enough yet, rather than your not having any capabilities to speak of. Know that we are all flawed, but that we also all have gifts to develop and to share. As you learn to know and accept yourself, you will find that it doesn't matter so much how other people treat you or perceive you. You will find that you are far less reactive to their perceptions of you, and more forgiving and accepting of both your flaws and weaknesses and those of people around you. You will begin to be far more dynamic in pursuing a better life for yourself and those you care about.

As you consider pursuing that rewarding life, the next chapter presents a most crucial step: creating your vision. How important is having a vision? The Bible puts it rather succinctly: *Where there is no vision, the people perish.* The flip side of that is, *with* a vision, you yourself, and those around you, can prosper.

3 Create Your Vision

I always knew that fury was my natural enemy. It clotted my blood and clogged my pores. It literally blinded me.

Maya Angelou

Sometimes you hear that people "stumble into success," that they got there by "blind luck." I don't agree with this theory. People may come upon an opportunity that surprises them; something might open up for them without any of their planning or doing. But the people who *take* those opportunities and *make* something of them are the ones who are successful. And they are successful because they have a vision for what they can do, given that opportunity that they've come across, and for what they can *be.*

So you can create your vision beforehand, with careful thought and planning, or you can create it as you come upon new opportunities. But either way, to be successful, you need to create it, because you can't sustain success for long without that vision.

Vision can begin with desire, but it doesn't end there. You can't just *want* something for yourself; you have to have a clear vision of how to *get* it. It's easy enough to dream about a better future for yourself, but you have to go beyond that. In this chapter we'll help you create your vision as we cover what it means to

- Have a vision for your life,
- Decide where you want to go, and
- Create your vision step by step.

In doing so, you'll learn to use your dreams to fuel your vision, and you'll learn to set goals, stay focused, and enjoy the journey.

Having a Vision for Your Life

As a teenager, I had the distractions that all kids face, but I stayed out of trouble because my parents let me know they expected more of me. Gang membership held no allure for me. I had better things to look ahead to. In those years, I had a vision of getting an athletic scholarship to college and going on to professional basketball. That vision kept me on track. I knew of good kids from good families in my town who somewhere took the wrong turn into dead-end lives. We all know of people we grew up with who had promise but threw it away. I know more than a handful of people who fell into lives of crime and drugs. Some went to prison. Some went to an early grave.

> Kids join gangs because that is all they see for themselves.

Those who choose the way of the street do so because they have a limited vision of where their lives can go. Kids don't join gangs because they don't want to be doctors or computer analysts or teachers or actors or businesspeople. They join gangs because that is all they see for themselves. Their vision for their lives is severely limited. Contrast this limited vision with the vision of Eric, who lives in a neighborhood surrounded by gang activity:

I have an older brother in prison right now. I told myself that's not the road I'm taking. I don't want to end up there. I want to make something of my life. I'm enrolling in junior college next year and plan to eventually get a bachelor's degree in education. I'd like to be a teacher because I want to make a difference in kids' lives, maybe get to them before they end up like my brother.

Eric, age 18

Even if it doesn't lead to gang membership or crime, a lack of a vision for where you want to go in life hurts your growth as a person. Remember how we defined vision in chapter 1? It's seeing your purpose in life, what you can *envision* yourself doing with your talents and desires. You cannot be successful if you have no vision or if you don't feel worthy of success. Having a vision for your life allows you to live out of hope rather than fear. In the next worksheet we'll begin to look at the issues that will help you create your vision. Your vision will begin to emerge as you think about what you most enjoy doing and what talents you most enjoy using.

■ Building on Pleasures and Talents

What do you like doing most? Why?

_____

_____

_____

_____

What gives your life meaning? When do you feel most energized, alive?

_____

_____

_____

_____

In a worksheet in the previous chapter, you noted areas where you feel competent and capable. Refer to that worksheet and then list five talents that you enjoy using.

1. _____

2. _____

3. _____

4. _____

5. _____

Now select the single talent that is your best, or that is most important to you. Don't worry if you feel you haven't "perfected" that talent; you have the rest of your life to keep improving it. This talent is central to your goals.

If you have two talents that are really important to you, simply choose one over the other for the sake of this exercise. That doesn't mean you won't develop the other talent, too.

_____

_____

Now think about the many ways that you can use that talent to improve your life. List ten ways that you can use your talent to improve your Success Circles (Career, Personal Development, and Relationships, or other areas of importance to you). Include things you are already doing with this talent and add things you can envision yourself doing in the future as you grow that talent.

1. _____

2. _____

3. _____

4. _____

5. _____

6. _____

7. _____

8. _____

9. _____

10. _____

From this list, what would you keep doing the rest of your life even if you didn't get paid for it?

_____

_____

_____

_____

Deciding Where You Want to Go

There's a saying that goes something like this: "If you don't know where you want to go, you'll probably end up someplace else." Once out of school, the average person changes *careers*—not just *jobs* within the same field—several times before settling in. Why? Because most people don't really know what they want to do with their lives. You ask them about their *vision* and they start talking about their last visit to the eye doctor. No matter what their eyesight is, their vision for their life is blurred at best.

Think of people you know who seem to be truly happy with their lives. I'll bet that they are doing what they want to do, living within the vision they chose for their lives. I know that I have never been happier than when I am working on my dreams and visions for a good life. It energizes me because I know exactly where I want to go. This is what Stephen Covey, author of *7 Habits of Highly Effective People,* refers to as "beginning with the end in mind." If you know where you want to go, you can start your journey with confidence and purpose.

I have seen what happens to people who lack a vision for bettering their lives. When I worked for the federal prison system, I saw hundreds of men who had no such vision. They had no guidelines for their lives, no idea of how to fit within society. Most broke early in their lives from the framework of society because they were never taught how to fit in, or how the process worked. They never saw a connection to success, and so instead they connected to failure.

> If you grow up knowing nothing other than gangs and street life, odds are that is where you will end up, unless you develop a greater vision.

If you grow up knowing nothing other than gangs and street life, odds are that is where you will end up, unless you develop a greater vision either on your own, or with the help of someone who wants a better life for you.

Imagine a neighborhood with rundown apartments lined with unkempt lawns and dead bushes. There is no real yard to play in. The only form of activity available to kids is a weathered cement basketball court with a few chain links acting as a hoop. The make-believe walls protect the players from the real world outside . . . the drug dealing and gang activity . . .

That is how NBA All-Star Larry Johnson, a member of Athletes Against Drugs, describes his childhood world when he gives speeches for AAD.

Larry grew up in South Dallas. It was a tough, stripped-down environment, but fortunately for him, he had a mother devoted to seeing him pursue a better life; he had athletic ability, and he had a vision that kept him off the streets and out of the violent world of gang membership. "Setting goals is the key to staying drug- and alcohol-free," Larry says. "Whether you want to be a fireman or a politician, once you know what you want out of life you will make sure nothing gets in the way of achieving success. You must focus on what it takes to get you where you want to be."

To get where you want to be, you need to take the proper route along the way. In the next worksheet, you'll consider the benefits of seeing the end before you take your first step on that journey.

■ Seeing the End Before You Begin

Describe a time when you began something with an end in mind. Did having the end in mind—in other words, the goal—help you? How?

_____

_____

_____

_____

_____

Describe a time when you got into trouble or when you performed poorly in something because you didn't consider the end—your goal—but just plunged headlong into it. How might things have been different if you'd had the end in mind?

_____

_____

_____

_____

Students who excel in school and life take responsibility for their lives. That is, they "take care of business" in the areas that are important to their success. In academics that means studying for however long it takes. In sports that means taking extra batting practice in baseball, or shooting fifty free throws in basketball after practice is over. In music that means practicing over and over until the music becomes part of you and flows naturally from you. Being responsible means knowing what your goal is and then taking the steps to make sure you reach your goal.

What are ways that you take responsibility for your life?

_____

_____

_____

_____

How does taking responsibility help you get where you want to go?

49

_____

_____

_____

_____

Creating Your Vision Step by Step

TEENS CAN MAKE IT HAPPEN

In the rest of this chapter we'll take you through six key steps to creating your vision:

- Taking inventory,
- Using your imagination,
- Setting goals,
- Identifying role models and mentors,
- Staying focused, and
- Enjoying the journey.

Step One: Take Inventory

What gives meaning and joy to your life? How can you find a way to make your life an expression of that joy? Let's say you like to sing. You might not land a huge record contract when you get out of school, but you can still sing as a way of life, whether as a professional performer or teacher, or in the church choir; or you could work within the industry to help others develop or market their talents. There are a lot of ways to approach your dream.

Your talents are your gifts. When you express those gifts, the world opens up to you. If you develop your talents, people and resources will come to you. And I believe that the true meaning of success is using your talents and abilities—your gifts—to better not only your life, but the lives of those around you.

Many people think that a talent has to be so pronounced that it hits them over the head, and if it doesn't, they say, "I don't have any talents." But the truth is, often you express your talents so naturally that you may not recognize them. What you love to do is generally what you naturally do well and what you have been doing all your life.

For instance, nurses are usually naturally nurturing people. Teachers and coaches enjoy sharing knowledge and helping young people develop. Business managers are well-organized people with leadership qualities. Salesmen are perceptive and have strong "people" skills. Comedians help us see the lighter side and help us laugh at ourselves.

You may not have a gift or special ability such as singing, or writing, or acting, or playing sports. Everyone, however, has some special ability or keen interest that can be developed, whether it is a knack for doing mechanical things, for building things, or for working well with other people. In the next worksheet you'll consider a few questions that help you determine your special ability or gift or interest—your purpose.

Your talents are your gifts. When you express those gifts, the world opens up to you.

■ Thinking on Purpose

Ask yourself what it is that you enjoy doing most. What gives your life meaning?

_____

_____

_____

Why do you think it is so meaningful to you?

_____

_____

_____

What do you look forward to doing more than anything else?

_____

_____

_____

51

What is it that you would do with your life even if you didn't get paid for it?

_____

_____

_____

Step Two: Use Your Imagination

So you've begun to focus on the talents and interests you want to pursue. What next? You do what a child does during play: *You use your imagination to create your reality.*

As children, we're usually wildly imaginative, but as we grow older, we sometimes lose our ability to imagine. We forget the importance of seeing the possibilities with our minds. Our minds become cluttered, busy, and too overwhelmed to see the way children see. We use our imagination less and less, and soon we find we have little imagination left. Believe me when I say that a strong imagination isn't just for children: It's for the most successful adults as well.

So should you fantasize about finding a pot of gold on your doorstep? No. Fantasies are frivolous dreams. They can be fun but they are dangerous if you spend so much time fantasizing that you neglect reality. Focus on dreaming within the realm of your experience. If you're planning to major in accounting in college, it does little good for you to fantasize about becoming a multimillionaire as soon as you graduate. Why? Because you're fantasizing about the goal without envisioning the process. It is far better to imagine the steps you'll need to take, from high school graduate to college student to college graduate to certified public accountant and on through the executive or entrepreneurial ranks.

Grown-ups, particularly athletes and artists, refer to this as the *visualization process.* Great quarterbacks say that they can "see" the proper receiver get open and catch a pass before it is even thrown. Artists talk about visualizing the finished work before they have begun it. To dream is different from fantasizing. To dream is to envision the possibility of something that is not only desirable, but attainable, based on who you are, and where you can go in life. By allowing yourself to dream within that context, you can create a new reality and new possibilities for your life.

What if your talent and interests lie in writing? You might consider magazine or newspaper journalism; television news writing; playwriting; teaching literature or creative writing; or writing fiction or nonfiction, newsletters, or advertising copy. There are many applications for most interests and talents. I know of a Chicago man whose interests include law, writing, and marketing. He didn't go to law school so he couldn't be a lawyer. He felt he couldn't support his

> To dream is different from fantasizing. To dream is to envision the possibility of something that is not only desirable, but attainable, based on who you are, and where you can go in life.

family by working as a writer. And he was unable to find a job he liked in marketing. But he is now very happy in his job as head of marketing for a law firm.

Refer to the worksheet earlier in this chapter in which you listed ten ways that you can use your talents to improve your Success Circles. Many of these things are within the realm of possibility for you, aren't they? Get in the habit of regularly thinking of the possibilities for you and your talents. Open your mind and expand your vision of where those talents can take you and how you can build your life around doing what you love to do. To truly add to the quality of your life, your vision has to be built around the things that you enjoy doing, and that you have a passion for.

In the next worksheet you'll use your imagination to form your vision.

■ Imagine That!

In earlier worksheets you've explored the areas in which you're confident, competent, and capable; the talents you most enjoy using and ways to grow those talents; beginning with the end in mind; and what gives your life meaning. Those worksheets lead naturally to this one, where you draw on that understanding of yourself to create your vision.

Based on your talents and interests and what you find meaningful, what are some careers that you are considering? Here are some examples: education, medicine, business, law, engineering, government, technology, sales, entertainment, media, and so on. List as many choices as you want, and beside each choice write what is most attractive to you about that choice.

_____

_____

_____

_____

_____

_____

If you listed more than three fields, now list your top three fields.

1. _____

2. _____

3. _____

Based on what you said in an earlier worksheet about what it is that you would do even if you didn't get paid for it, pick one field. This field should have possibilities in it for you that would allow you to do that one thing.

_____

_____

_____

Within that field, list jobs or areas that you would be interested in.

_____

_____

_____

Knowing yourself as you do, especially after having worked through previous worksheets, complete the following sentence. This should be answered at the gut level, without overanalyzing yourself.

If I could really do whatever I wanted in life, I would be a . . .

_____

_____

_____

Realize that this worksheet doesn't limit you to one career field or choice; these decisions will evolve as you continue to develop and grow. This worksheet is meant to help you begin to consider your possibilities. Use it as a guidepost for now. In the next section we'll talk about goals—and how you have to be flexible in adapting them as you go along.

Step Three: Setting Goals

Once you have developed your vision, set goals to serve as stepping stones toward fulfilling your vision. Goals help you focus on where you want to be each step of your journey so that as you proceed, you can determine your progress toward fulfilling your vision.

As you set goals, keep these eight guidelines in mind:

1. *Goals should be realistic.*

Don't waste your time setting unrealistic goals. You don't reach unrealistic goals, and then you feel discouraged, thinking you've failed. What

you've really failed at is setting realistic goals. Let's put it in terms not of any career path, but of an immediate goal while you're in high school. Let's say you love music and you want to play in a rock or jazz band. You've dabbled a little bit with guitar; you took lessons several years ago. But to say you're rusty is being kind. If your goal is to go out and join a band, then you're setting yourself up for failure. No band is going to want to take someone on who is just learning. But if your goal is to take more lessons and practice and make great improvement over the next several months, and *then* maybe join a band, now that's a realistic goal.

2. *Goals should be meaningful.*

Focus your goals on your vision. Don't set goals that lead you nowhere in particular. If you set goals that have no real meaning for your life, you may not achieve the goals, and even if you do, they won't get you closer to living the type of life that is truly meaningful to you. You can set a goal to get better grades; but if you're not planning to go to college, chances are that goal won't have much meaning for you, and you probably won't reach the goal. If, as you consider your future, you expand your vision to include college, then grades suddenly become meaningful to you. They are the means to a better end, and you're much more likely to improve your grades.

3. *Goals should be well defined.*

When you set out on a trip you don't generally say, "Sometime soon, I think I'll go a couple hundred miles to the northeast somewhere and get there when I get there." No, you set a specific destination and a specific time when you want to be there. When you set goals in your journey to a better life, you want them also to be well defined. "I want to make a lot of money," may well be part of your vision, but it is not a well-defined goal. Neither is, "I am going to work for the benefit of mankind." Instead, well-defined goals might be, "I'm going to get straight As my senior year and study hard for the college entrance exams so I can get into the college of my choice," or "I'm going to volunteer to help at summer camp this summer."

4. *Goals should excite* You.

I put the emphasis on *you* because this is your vision for your life. People around you may have good intentions and you should certainly listen to and consider their advice; but don't let them throw you off the path by allowing them to set goals for you that are more in line with their vision than yours.

5. *Goals should follow a logical progression.*

This is the old don't-put-the-cart-before-the-horse warning. Your goals should be step by step so they make perfect sense and so that you always know, out of pure logic, that the next one is within reach and that it moves you toward your destination.

6. *Goals may need fine-tuning.*

Realistically, things can happen as you pursue your vision of a better life, so your goals may require fine-tuning along the way. You may accomplish some goals easier than you had thought while others may elude you. Keep your vision in mind and adjust as you go, to stay on target.

Things change. A good running back in football, hopeful of a college scholarship, tears up his knee. A teenage pianist who has won awards in competitions and has always dreamed of being a performer discovers the joy of *teaching* piano and decides to go that route instead. A streetwise kid is introduced to the ins and outs of managing a business during an informal "internship" and finds, to his amazement, that he loves it!

The teen years, as you know, are times of turbulent change. Expect change to happen, expect your feelings and interests to change, and adjust your goals accordingly. The important thing is to keep goals ahead of you at all times. Goals are not the ultimate reward. The reward is in pursuing the dream.

7. *Goals should require positive action.*

A primary purpose for setting goals is to get you moving in the right direction. There is really no reason to set goals that don't challenge you to take action. "I am going to consider losing some weight" is not a goal. "At 10 A.M. tomorrow I am going to jog three miles." That is a goal. Setting goals within each of your Success Circles, acting upon them, and achieving them not only moves you forward, it builds your confidence in your ability to pursue your vision of a rewarding life. Goals help you act on your dreams rather than just wishing or hoping for them.

8. *Goals should not isolate you.*

I know of a very smart person whose goal was to become a surgeon. He set his mind on that goal in high school and went after it. But he became so obsessed with his goal that he neglected most of the rest of his life. He never formed close relationships because they might have distracted him from his studies. He rarely went to family functions because he didn't want to fall behind in school.

He reached his goal of becoming a surgeon, but he has no life outside of his work; his life is one-dimensional. He is a lonely guy because he took care of business but he didn't take care of the rest of his life. Your relationships and your personal life are not secondary considerations. Goals should not be all-consuming and focused on one aspect of life; they should be part of a healthy life, addressing many aspects, helping you to be a more complete person.

Here's an example of how you can use goals to better your life: A few years ago, I received a letter from a Marquette University student from Chicago named Chris Janson. He was a marketing major and intensely interested in a career in sports marketing. He had seen my column on that subject in *Inside Sports* magazine and he was writing to see if my company had any internships or job openings.

Obviously, Chris had a vision for his life and he had set a goal within that vision of landing an entry-level job within his field of interest. I wrote Chris back and told him that I didn't have a position for him at that time, but that I'd be happy to talk to him anytime he wanted to come in. Chris responded by offering to work for me *for free* just to get some experience in the field and to make some contacts. Now here is a young man determined to go after his vision, I thought.

Needless to say, I gave Chris a call, invited him to come by, and put him on my staff as an intern. He did work for me in that position for a brief time for no pay, but only until I saw what potential he had; then I put him on a salary. He worked for me for nearly three years, and I have no doubt that some day he will have his own sports marketing firm.

Chris set a goal, acted on it, and changed his life. He should feel very good about that, and it should give him the confidence to set progressively bigger and more challenging goals for the rest of his life. When you identify goals consistent with your vision for a fulfilling life, you set a direction just as you would in choosing a destination to sail to on a boat. As any sailor knows, "If you do not know which harbor you are headed for, no wind is the right one." You set goals by understanding what you want to do and where you want to go.

You may come from a disadvantaged background. You may have low self-esteem. But you are free to dream of a better life and then to act upon that dream. There will be challenges in life; we all have our challenges. If you are going nowhere, there is no reason to take on those challenges, but if you have goals and a vision of where you want to go then you will be motivated to overcome the challenges. You may not overcome every challenge, but if you learn from each of them and hold on to your vision, it is almost impossible to be defeated.

In the following worksheet you'll get a chance to list your own goals that will help you pursue your vision for a better life.

■ Goals: The Game Plans of Life

For goals to be effective, they need to be built around some guiding principles—your values and beliefs. What values, beliefs, or principles matter most to you?

_____

_____

_____

The following list of values may help you identify your values or beliefs. Circle those that are meaningful to you.

Achievement	Financial security	Intimacy
Aesthetics	Friendship	Justice
Appearance	Genuineness	Knowledge
Beauty	Growth	Leisure
Career achievement	Health	Meaning
Creativity	Helping	New experiences
Dependability	Home	Physical comforts
Education	Honesty	Pleasure
Enjoyment	Influence	Possessions

Power	Security	Sharing
Prestige	Self-determination	Status
Purpose	Self-direction	Travel
Recognition	Self-respect	Wealth

The pope has goals; so does a car thief. The difference is in the quality of their vision and their focus. Go over the following questions when considering how your vision is going to be focused.

What do you want to accomplish in your life?

_____

_____

_____

_____

_____

Why do you want to achieve your goals? For example, will society or people around you benefit?

_____

_____

_____

_____

_____

Make a list of ten goals that will help you pursue your vision. Your goals should be in line with your talents and your values.

1. _____

2. _____

3. _____

4. _____

5. _____

6. _____

7. _____

8. _____

9. _____

10. _____

If you attain your goals or are on the road to attaining them, what will your life be like . . .

One year from now?

_____

_____

_____

Five years from now?

_____

_____

_____

Ten years from now?

_____

_____

_____

Step Four: Identifying Role Models and Mentors

A role model is someone you admire and would like to model parts of your life after. Sometimes a role model is someone you know—a parent, a brother or sister, an aunt or uncle, a teacher or coach, and so on. Sometimes a role model is someone you don't know personally, but you know enough about his or her life that you aspire to be like him or her.

A mentor, on the other hand, is an adult who acts as a trusted counselor or guide. Mentors can help you not only establish goals and pursue them, but they can offer you advice and encouragement along the way.

One of my guides, or mentors, is Bob Brown of Highpoint, North Carolina. Bob is widely known as a source of wisdom and guidance for African Americans seeking to make it in the business world. I met Bob at a social gathering back when I was just trying to get started in business. We started talking and I immediately liked him. I just gravitated toward him. It happens in life. If you are looking to better yourself, you will draw people like him to you.

Bob owns B&C Associates, an international public relations firm serving Fortune 500 clients and many very influential figures, particularly people in state and local government. When we first met, Bob made public relations and marketing sound fascinating. It is a field of relationships and contacts. It is a business that demands a high level of creativity and communication and people skills. It is also a field with a lot of wonderful opportunities. Bob introduced me to one of those opportunities when he invited me to accompany him on a trip to the Ivory Coast of Africa, where he was working with the government to attract business investors.

On the trip, Bob and I forged a friendship and he invited me to join his business; so I moved to North Carolina to work with him. My title was vice president of business development, but I was really a trainee. I was green and didn't know really what was going on, so I learned by traveling with Bob. Not that I learned it all, but I did establish a foundation of knowledge in the business.

Here's an example of a teenager who benefited from having a mentor:

I want to be a really great sportswriter, but when I started out I was really green. But my school newspaper adviser knew I was serious about it, so he introduced me when I was a junior to Mark Lyton, the sports editor of our hometown paper. Mr. Lyton took me under his wing—I did an internship with him for two summers at the paper. He took me to baseball games that he covered, including a couple of major league games, and I wrote my own articles and columns based on all the games I attended with him. He'd critique them and help me see what I was doing well and where I could improve. I even got to interview a few major league players, though mainly I let Mr. Lyton do the interviewing. I learned a lot about interviewing, and knowing what details to look for, what makes a good story, how to get that story, and how to write it both fast and well. Now I have a ton of confidence going into college and into journalism school. I feel light-years ahead of where I would have been without having the advice and encouragement from Mr. Lyton.

Jarret, age 18

In the next worksheet you'll identify any role models or mentors in *your* life. These are the people who can see your potential and who encourage you.

61

Mentors especially are important, because they can help you refine your vision for your life.

■ A Little Help From Your Mentors and Role Models

Make a list of the people who have helped you and how they have helped.

_____

_____

_____

_____

_____

_____

If you can't think of anyone, your problem may be that you have not clearly defined your vision for your life. Remember, you can't expect others to see it for you if you can't see it for yourself.

Now make a list of up to five people who could provide wisdom, guidance, and encouragement as you set goals. Make specific plans for contacting these people and for seeking their guidance.

1. _____

2. _____

3. _____

4. _____

5. _____

Consider the area or field in which you'd like to be mentored. What type of advice are you seeking?

_____

_____

_____

In your relationship with a mentor, what are your responsibilities? That is, given that he or she is there to help you, what can you do to help your mentor help you?

_____

_____

_____

How can you get the most out of a relationship with a mentor while not taking advantage of the mentor's time?

_____

_____

_____

Step Five: Staying Focused

Setting goals is one thing; staying focused on them is another—and often harder—thing to do. To be successful you have to follow through and stay focused in life. If not, you lose power and direction. It's not that you can't enjoy other aspects of your life, but those goals always have to be at the forefront. Successful people are focused and not easily distracted from their goals, whatever they are.

You will have distractions. You will have temptations. You will occasionally want to coast or take shortcuts even if they take you in the wrong direction. Keep that vision of a fulfilling life in your head. If you're a cross-country runner and your goal is to win your league championship, it does you no good to shave miles off your training runs. True, it may be easier, but it takes your focus off your goal and diminishes your chances of reaching that goal.

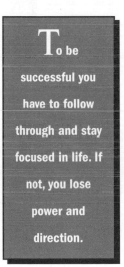

To be successful you have to follow through and stay focused in life. If not, you lose power and direction.

Step Six: Enjoying the Journey

As you work toward your goals, if you find yourself anxious and snapping at people, it may be a warning that you've wandered off track, or perhaps that your vision needs adjustment. Remember, this is a long journey, a life's journey, and you want to be able to savor and enjoy each step along the way.

Your vision should not be focused on making money or acquiring things. High living isn't the goal. Elevating others through your life is. The focus of your vision should be on developing and using your talents for the enjoyment and welfare of others as well as for the benefit of you and your loved ones. If you make a lot of money by allowing your talents to flourish, that's great, but making a lot of money shouldn't be your goal. Far too many people go to their graves with money in the bank but nothing in their hearts. Others lead far more fulfilling lives elevating the lives of those around them by using their talents and doing the things they love the most. School teachers certainly do not make enough money in relation to the importance of their role in society, particularly at a time when they have to not only teach, but instill values in so many children who may not get what they need at home. Nurses and social workers, policemen and firemen, and the people who make our cities work all contribute greatly to the quality of our lives without taking home huge paychecks.

Many of these people will tell you that they are doing what is most important to them, that they are filling a great need. You have to respect that sort of character. These are people who have created their lives based on something far more rewarding than material goods. They do what they do because it allows them to feel good about themselves. When you are creating a vision for a better life, that is important to keep in mind. What can you do that will allow you to feel good about yourself?

A successful life does not necessarily mean more money or a bigger house or vacations in Europe. A successful life can simply mean a life with meaning. A rewarding life. A life that contributes to the common good. A life that nurtures goodness in others.

That life will grow from your vision. But you need more than just a vision. You need a plan to make that vision a reality. And that's what we'll talk about in the next chapter.

4 Develop Your Travel Plan

If you don't know where you're going, you'll end up someplace else.

Yogi Berra

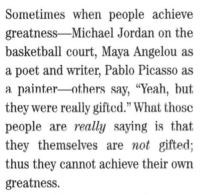

Sometimes when people achieve greatness—Michael Jordan on the basketball court, Maya Angelou as a poet and writer, Pablo Picasso as a painter—others say, "Yeah, but they were really gifted." What those people are *really* saying is that they themselves are *not* gifted; thus they cannot achieve their own greatness.

That statement is true—Jordan, Angelou, and Picasso *were* tremendously gifted. But they weren't handed success on a platter. Jordan, in fact, had quite ordinary skills as a youngster. He was cut—Michael Jordan was *cut!*—from his junior high basketball team. Maya Angelou was raped at the age of eight and, as a result of the mental trauma, was unable to speak for several years. The story is told of an art lover who watched Picasso create a painting in a few hours. The observer naively said how wonderful it must be to create a masterpiece in so short a time. Picasso reportedly replied, "You weren't here to watch the forty years of work that went into my art."

The truth is, we are *all* gifted; we *all* have the potential to achieve great things. But all too many of us don't tap deeply into that potential because we give up when the road gets rocky. Anyone can stroll down a clear, smooth lane. But when the road takes twists and turns, when it becomes bumpy and dips and climbs, when you can't see too far in the distance because your focus is necessarily on the difficult steps immediately ahead of you, do you keep on keeping on, or do you stop and look for the nearest exit?

No one's road to success is easy. It's been said that the two sure things in life are death and taxes. On the road to success, the two sure things are failure and doubt. You have to learn from the former and conquer the latter to achieve success. And to do so, you have to have a travel plan in mind for that bumpy road. The plan has to be well developed, grounded in your values, and coming from your vision for yourself.

Having a vision for what you want to be is essential, but it's not enough. You need a plan for making that vision happen. Michael Jordan didn't just stroll on his way toward six National Basketball Association championships. He put his physical gifts to use, but of perhaps even greater importance, he had a fierce, unrelenting determination to succeed. In fact, in his later years in the NBA, he was known less for his individual skills and more for his unparalleled ability to lead, to *will* his team to win, to face and triumph over adversity again and again. He had a vision, and he had a definite plan in mind to make that vision a reality.

Creating visions, developing travel plans to achieve those visions, and experiencing success doesn't just happen to adults. It happens to youngsters in every venue: academics, art, music, writing, sports, achievement clubs, you name it. Don't think only in terms of your *future* success. Think in terms of success *now*. If you want to win a regional piano competition, if you want to earn National Honor Society honors, if you want to publish short stories or poems before you graduate, if you want to win a league or state title in wrestling, what do you have to do? What steps do you have to take? You'd be amazed at what you can make happen when you set your mind to it. But it doesn't just happen because you *want* it to happen. It happens because you *plan* to make it happen.

That's what this chapter is all about: planning to make it happen. In this chapter we'll help you turn your vision into reality by

- Choosing action steps toward your goals,
- Making time for goals and for all aspects of life,
- Getting and keeping on schedule,
- Evaluating your progress, and
- Staying focused on what's truly important.

The journey in making your vision become a reality can often seem daunting. But there is a path, there is a way, to make it happen. The key is to plan to take the right steps to help you achieve what you want. And then you take those steps, one step at a time.

Taking One Step at a Time

Whether you're a wrestler planning to win a league title next season, or a student with an entrepreneurial bent who wants to start your own business and build a successful career, you need to plan the right steps. And don't get caught up thinking that any success you experience as a student has no bearing on, or relationship to, future success in the "real" world. You *are* in the "real" world—*your* world. Success now breeds success later, even if the fields or venues change. Don't discount what you might consider "small" successes. Michael Jordan's first step to basketball success was making his high school team after being cut earlier. Your successes—however great or small—in academics, social clubs, fine arts, or sports can pave the way to future success. What's important at the moment is not how much you achieve, but how much you learn about the process of achieving. Because once you learn the process, you can apply it in the field or area of your choice, where you want to use the gifts you have.

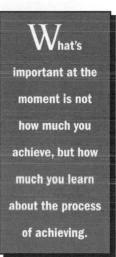

What's important at the moment is not how much you achieve, but how much you learn about the process of achieving.

There really are no shortcuts to lifelong success. Some people become overnight successes, but often they fade as fast as they came on the scene. How many singers or bands are known as "one-hit wonders"? How many athletes succeed in professional sports without first spending years developing their skills? Often, the reason people fail after "one hit" or a brief period of success is that they weren't prepared for long-term success. They didn't build a foundation of knowledge and training and experience.

Don't plan for overnight success; plan for long-term success. Whatever your goals, don't rush at them. Identify those actions that will move you toward your goals as efficiently as possible. Once you spend time it is gone, so you don't want to waste your time on steps that don't contribute to your progress toward your goals. If you want to be a great writer, you won't achieve success by starting out with a single thought or line and then expecting the Great American Novel to flow from that. Great novelists sometimes go to excruciating lengths preparing to write. They create characters with back stories that will never reach the printed page so that they know exactly how the character will act or react in various situations. They devise plots that continuously move the story forward and create tension—and thus reader interest—by continually placing the main characters in jeopardy of achieving their goals. They construct extensive outlines. They read widely, observe how people speak and act, and are constantly thinking in terms of the type of detail and description that will enrich their story, give it life, make it flow. Great novelists, in essence, never stop working, though they may go for many weeks without putting pen to paper (or fingertips to keyboard). They don't rush greatness; they cultivate it and nourish it. The writing of a great novel is the culmination of a lot of work that took place before the first word was written.

And so it must be with you. You must cultivate your own success, taking the necessary steps along the way. Sometimes these steps are mundane and unexciting; often they are painful and filled with drudgery. For every Olympic athlete's shining moment, there are thousands of hours of practice away from the spotlight. But those shining moments are never achieved without a specific plan in mind and the perseverance to stick to that plan, because it is the way to achieve the goal.

> I did really poorly in regionals the year before. I was pretty depressed. But after a little while I made a plan and set some goals—not to win state, but to improve my performance. I set some really high goals and I knew what it would take. I worked hard all year long. Still, I was surprised—I wasn't expecting a championship. I just wanted to reach my goal.
>
> Sue, age 17, state swimming champion

Each of us has limited time, energy, and resources, so it is not possible to do everything that might move us toward our goals. Deciding which steps to take can be difficult, but if you weigh your choices carefully, you can make great strides with a few efficient steps rather than running all over the place trying to do too much. Effective planning involves prioritizing those steps that move you most efficiently toward your goal.

For many of you, simply reading this book or being part of a Success Club is one small action taken toward fulfilling a vision for a fulfilling life. The fact that you have begun to take action may have already brought about subtle changes in the way you live your life. When you set goals and achieve them by following a plan, you create a certain *magic* by building confidence in your own value and worthiness. You begin to live out of your imagination, looking forward to the possibilities for your life rather than backward at the limitations and liabilities of your past.

When you begin to actually work toward your goals through a plan of action, you assert power over your life. You prove that you have control. When you live life with purpose and energy by acting upon goals that are based in principles that you believe in, then you are living on your full power. You are fully engaged in life. You know who you are and where you are going and what sort of person you want to be when you get there.

How do you develop a plan? Step by step; one foot in front of the other; following the route that best serves your purposes, whether it is along a well-traveled highway over the river and through the woods, or along untraveled terrain. Selecting the route that is right for you is critical. You don't rush the planning stage of your life's journey any more than you would take off on a long trip without studying the map first to determine the best route for your purposes.

Note that I wrote *for your purposes.* You and I may both be driving to Atlanta from Chicago but you may have relatives in Chattanooga who would be hurt if you didn't stop by. I may have an old army buddy in Nashville I'd like to visit. It might be easier if we could all follow the same plan for pursuing our goals, but the fact is, each of us is unique. We each have our own talents, strengths, weaknesses, goals, and vision for our lives. That is why it is so important to take your time to consider all of your options and to select those that are best for you.

As a simple example, let's say you are a track athlete and your season has just ended; summer is fast approaching. Your goal is to win your conference 1,600-meter title next spring. What are some steps you can take toward your goal?

1. Make a vow that you believe in yourself and that you will keep your commitment to your goal.
2. Share your goal with your coach and tell him or her you want to do whatever it takes in training to reach your goal.
3. Read magazine articles and books on training and consult with your coach on the type of training you need to do on your own over the summer.
4. Do the training over the summer.
5. Incorporate weight training to strengthen your upper body and improve your running form.
6. Eat healthful foods to fuel your training and to be healthy.
7. Develop or maintain other healthy habits, such as getting enough sleep, listening to your body when it's telling you to back off from training or risk injury, and abstaining from tobacco, alcohol, and other drugs.
8. Read books and articles on mental toughness and mental imagery to improve the mental aspects of your running.
9. Run road races in the summer and cross-country in the fall to keep sharp and to improve race tactics.
10. Stay focused and positive in down times during your training, and in setbacks in early races.

11. Focus on speed endurance and speed training as the conference meet approaches.
12. Always believe in yourself. Constantly envision yourself winning the conference title, employing the strategy that best suits you.

Taking these steps will move you toward your goal of winning the conference championship.

■ Action Steps Toward Your Goals

Now let's consider the ten goals you listed on pages 59–60 in chapter 3. Choose one of those ten goals. Write your goal here:

_____

_____

_____

Now write down ten actions that will help you reach your goal. Don't worry about putting them in chronological order or in order of importance; just list ten steps. If you need help, ask a friend, a teacher, or one of your family members to help you brainstorm about actions you might take to move toward your goals.

1. _____
2. _____
3. _____
4. _____
5. _____
6. _____
7. _____
8. _____
9. _____
10. _____

Now identify three of these ten actions that are most likely to help you achieve your goal. Write the three actions and rank them in order of most important to least important.

1. _____

2. _____

3. _____

You now have identified three important steps to take in reaching your goal. And you have begun to learn the process of developing a travel plan.

Think about your plan for reaching your goal and search for someone who had a similar goal. Study how that person did it. What initial steps did that person take? What worked and what didn't work? Don't be afraid to go to that person and ask questions. You will probably be surprised to find that successful people are willing to share their success with others.

A tried-and-true method for accelerating your learning process is to seek out someone who has already traveled the road you have selected for your journey to a better life. The role model I selected to learn more about starting my own business was Cleveland lawyer Mark H. McCormack, founder of International Management Group, a pioneering sports management and marketing company.

Back in the early 1960s, McCormack was just a young lawyer looking for a way to combine his business with his love of golf. He created his vision around something he enjoyed doing, just as I advised you to do in the previous chapter. With an initial investment of only $500 and a wealth of common sense and street smarts, he built a billion-dollar international business that represents more than six hundred athletes around the world. IMG not only manages the careers of athletes, it also conducts sporting and special events, produces television programming, does marketing for Fortune 500 firms, offers financial planning for top corporate executives, and consults for the Olympics.

> A tried-and-true method for accelerating your learning process is to seek out someone who has already traveled the road you have selected for your journey to a better life.

I studied the operations of IMG and have implemented many of McCormack's methods and tactics. A formal education provides you with a great foundation to build upon, but it is hard to beat real-world experience. If you find someone who is doing what you think you may want to do with your life, you might even consider working for this role model, perhaps as a summer intern, in order to speed up your own progress.

Getting—and Keeping—on Track

Determining what actions to take to best pursue your goals is only the first step in enacting your plan. The second step is setting up a schedule to take those actions. Time management experts generally agree that the best thing to do is set up a weekly schedule. Scheduling, they say, is the bridge between knowing what to do and doing it.

When you schedule yourself to do something by picking an exact time to do it, it motivates you to get the task done. A band instructor doesn't say to his or her students, "Just drop by some time and we'll practice." A car mechanic doesn't say, "Oh, just drop it off and I'll get to it one of these days." When you really want something done, you pick a definite time and you get it done. It's all in how you manage time.

Time management is a major issue for teens and adults alike. I'm going to describe four common causes of poor time management, and then you'll do a worksheet on time management skills.

- *Cause #1:* The first cause of poor time management is *procrastination.* You operate under the mistaken belief that you will have time later to do a task, and you never get to it.
- *Cause #2:* Another cause of poor time management is being unrealistic about how much you can get done, so you always bite off more than you can chew.
- *Cause #3:* A third cause is called *task creeping.* Before you are able to complete a task, you agree to take on another one. This happens again and again until you are overloaded and can't tend effectively to anything you have taken on.
- *Cause #4:* The fourth cause, related to the third cause, is jumping from one task to another, either from lack of concentration, inability to prioritize tasks, or impending deadlines. The result is you are able to complete none of the tasks very satisfactorily.

You need to be realistic about taking on new tasks or projects and about how much time you have to give to them, and you have to be wise in scheduling your time to accomplish your goals for tasks or projects not only effectively, but in a timely manner. Wasting time, or putting things off, or jumping from one thing to another, won't get it done. You need to be a wise scheduler of your time.

▣ Time To Plan

How effective are you at planning your time? Complete this worksheet, total your points, and then see the scale at the end.

1. How often do you plan your day or your week in advance?

Always	1
Frequently	2
Sometimes	3
Seldom	4
Never	5

73

2. How often do you procrastinate on tasks you know you need to get done?

Never	1
Seldom	2
Sometimes	3
Frequently	4
Always	5

3. How often do you feel so stressed that you "just don't have enough time" to accomplish a task?

Never	1
Seldom	2
Sometimes	3
Frequently	4
Always	5

4. How often do you waste time in unproductive conversations and meetings?

Never	1
Seldom	2
Sometimes	3
Frequently	4
Always	5

5. To what extent does your schedule allow time for the unexpected?

Always	1
Frequently	2
Sometimes	3
Seldom	4
Never	5

6. How often do you agree to take on another task before completing the task you were working on?

Never	1
Seldom	2
Sometimes	3
Frequently	4
Always	5

7. How often do you find yourself rushing through tasks for various projects, completing none of them to your satisfaction, because you don't have time to do so?

Never	1
Seldom	2
Sometimes	3
Frequently	4
Always	5

8. How often do you jump from task to task because you're not sure how to prioritize them?

Never	1
Seldom	2
Sometimes	3
Frequently	4
Always	5

9. How often do you lose a good idea because you were busy doing something else and didn't have time to write it down?

Never	1
Seldom	2
Sometimes	3
Frequently	4
Always	5

10. How often do you find yourself saying yes to a task or project when your schedule is already filled, because you want to be involved in the new task or project?

Never	1
Seldom	2
Sometimes	3
Frequently	4
Always	5

Score:

10 to 15–Excellent
16 to 20–Very good
21 to 25–Good
26 to 30–Okay
31 to 50–Poor

How did you score? If you didn't score so well, pay special attention to the next section on how to improve your time management skills.

Improving Your Time Management Skills

Don't feel too bad if you didn't score high on your time management worksheet. Managing time is a skill that most of us need to continually work at. In today's fast-paced world, most people feel they have less free time than they used to, and more things to tend to. As a result, they always feel they're in a "time crunch." Thus the need to develop and improve your time management skills is crucial to your ability to plan and accomplish the goals you've set.

Rainer Martens, author of *Successful Coaching* (Updated Second Edition), provides these tips for managing time:

- Plan your time regularly.
- Clearly define your immediate goals and then write weekly plans. Review these plans at least once a day and mark off tasks that you've accomplished.
- Set realistic goals. Goals can be high, but not impossible to achieve.
- Be realistic in how much you take on, and in how much time you allot for each task.
- Prioritize tasks and estimate how much time each will take. Always give your attention to the tasks that *must* be done.
- Don't take on more tasks unless you know you'll have time for them after you complete the tasks that you *must* do.
- Develop concentration skills. To effectively accomplish tasks in the time allotted, you'll need to concentrate.
- Eliminate all the self-distractions that you can as you work on your task. Focus on one thing at a time.
- Write down important thoughts or notes related to the task. Don't rely on your memory.
- Set and keep deadlines.
- Delegate tasks to others when possible; stick to the work that you truly must do. If you're on a committee or in a club, don't feel compelled to do others' work for them.
- Encourage others not to waste your time. Learn how to close conversations when they're hampering your ability to get something done.
- Slow down and regroup when you feel overwhelmed. Revisit your goals and your plans and prioritize your work.
- Find time for yourself. Have some healthy outlets; this will help you manage stress and time.

Accepting the Messiness of Life

When planning your week, don't think of school, personal, social, and family activities as separate. They aren't. Things happen in each aspect of your life that affect other aspects. If you're having problems with your parents, or if your parents are going through a separation or divorce, your schoolwork will likely be affected. If your days have become hectic with school projects, club commitments, practices, and so on, your personal life and your time for relating to your family and friends who aren't involved in these activities will be affected. On the flip side, if you have strong relationships at home and with good friends, this can provide stability and help you manage even during stressful times.

> You can't put the various aspects of your life into neat compartments. It just doesn't work that way. One thing spills over into another.

The point is, you can't put the various aspects of your life into neat compartments. It just doesn't work that way. One thing spills over into another. When you are growing in your school life, that tends to spur growth in your personal life, and vice versa. If you want to schedule an activity that moves you closer to your academic or career goals, there is no reason why that activity can't also contribute to your goals for your personal development or family life. Certainly this applies in physical activity, which can benefit all aspects of your life. But even if the activity is just going to the library to do some research, it is still possible to take along a family member who might enjoy the trip and take the opportunity to share something with you.

Your weekly activities don't have to just be things that you do. They can be things that you learn, or seek to understand, or share. If you are trying to choose your field of study that you are considering pursuing in college, one of your week's activities might be to talk to someone who is in one of those fields and can tell you what it is like.

Next you'll do a worksheet that helps you plan your steps toward reaching a goal.

■ Making Time to Take Action

In a worksheet earlier in this chapter (entitled "Action Steps Toward Your Goals"), you identified the three actions that would most help you achieve a particular goal. Review those three actions that you wrote down and write them again in the space below.

Action #1 _____

Action #2 _____

Action #3 _____

Now schedule those actions for a specific time on a specific day next week.

I will complete these activities at the following times:

Action # 1: Day of week/Date _____ Time _____

Action # 2: Day of week/Date _____ Time _____

Action # 3: Day of week/Date _____ Time _____

Now there's only one thing left to do: take action!

Checking Your Progress

Scheduling action is a commitment you make to yourself. And reviewing your schedule can reinforce your sense that you are in control of your life. It is also important to evaluate how each week went in order to learn from your experiences and to help you see what is working for you and what isn't.

You might want to do each evaluation on the back of your weekly schedules or in a separate journal. Here are some suggestions for questions to ask yourself each week to monitor your progress toward your goals.

As you review the questions, be honest with yourself. You won't learn anything if you deceive yourself or make excuses. The whole idea behind an evaluation is to consider what went well, what was difficult, and how you might improve. A self-evaluation is to keep you on track or help you get on track.

- Which activities moved you most effectively toward your goal?
- What difficulties did you experience?
- How did you deal with these difficulties?
- Which activities were not helpful?
- Did having scheduled activities help you stay focused and motivated?
- Were you able to coordinate school activities with family, social, and personal activities?
- What beliefs, values, or principles came into play during the week?
- Were any of those beliefs, values, or principles challenged, compromised, or set aside?
- How did this week measure up against others as far as activities that moved you toward your goals?

- Do your goals and your vision for your life still appear to be realistic? Challenging? Worthwhile?
- Are you asking too much of yourself? Not enough?
- Is there any problem or obstacle that seems to be appearing on a regular basis?
- Is there anything about your plan that needs improvement? Your motivation?

Staying Focused on Your Vision

You've probably seen photographs of carriage horses in Central Park in New York, along Michigan Avenue in Chicago, or in other cities around the world. Many of them wear blinders that allow them to see only where they are supposed to be going. The blinders block out distractions so that they keep on going in the right direction. That's what you need to do in pursuing your dreams and your vision. There are four keys to remember when you set out to pursue your vision for your life:

1. It is just as important to know what *not* to do as what to do.
2. Don't allow yourself to be distracted from the truly important things in your journey by the *urgent* things that cry out to you.
3. Don't procrastinate.
4. Every day, do something that is truly important in moving you toward your goals.

We'll go briefly into each key.

Knowing What *Not* to Do

It is just as important to know what not *to do as what to do.* Don't back down when faced with challenges or hard times as you follow your vision, but don't waste time on things you cannot control or that don't move you closer to your goals. For some of you this may mean making wiser decisions about how you spend your time and whom you spend it with. For others it may mean letting go of things that bother you but that you can't change. Focus on the things that you can change and actions that you can take in order to achieve your goals.

Problems outside your control often are related to something that has happened in the past. You can only influence your current and future behavior, so you should not waste your time worrying about something that is in the past. This is reflected in the Serenity Prayer: "Lord, grant me the power to accept the things that

I cannot change, the courage to change the things I can, and the wisdom to know the difference."

> **F**ocus on the things that you can change and actions that you can take in order to achieve your goals.

I had this big algebra final that I was really psyched about, because I had worked hard all semester. Algebra doesn't come that easily to me, but I figured I had a chance to ace it because I was going to really study hard in the last couple of weeks before the test.

Then Kenny tells me he's going to prom with Angela. I couldn't believe it! This was my senior prom, and he had asked me two months ago. I had my dress and everything. I was really, really ticked off! I figured I should just forget it—he wasn't worth the anger—but I was too upset. I couldn't stop thinking about it, and I couldn't study. I got a C on the test. When I looked at my grade on the test I thought two things: First I thought, Kenny, you jerk. Look what happened because of you. Then I thought, you know, it's my fault. I let him get to me. He's not the one who had the test to take.

Lisa, age 17

Don't be like Lisa. Put things in the past that should be there, and focus on the present, on what you can control.

Keeping Your Priorities Straight

Don't be distracted from the truly important things in your journey by the urgent things that cry out to you. For example, it might be *important* that you get your American Lit paper done within a few days, so you have to put off the *urgent* things such as socializing with your friends or talking over serious matters with your girlfriend or boyfriend.

Have you ever had the experience of looking back and wondering why you paid attention to certain "urgent" things in your life, when you should have been tending to things that were truly more important? As they say, hindsight is 20/20. The irony is that the urgent things in your life tug at your sleeves, shout, stamp their feet, whistle, do anything to get your attention, while the truly important things are in the background, waiting for *you* to come to them. They aren't going anywhere but they often aren't "in your face" the way urgent matters tend to be. And so it's easy to overlook the important things.

My little sister has always looked up to me, sort of idolized me. I mean, we have our fights, but we're really close. Well, she was so pumped, because she was starting on the varsity volleyball team as a sophomore. Her first match was on a Thursday night. She said, "Corey, you gotta be there, I'm so nervous, but if you're there I'll be okay." I knew she'd do fine but I was proud of her and couldn't wait to see her play.

Then Jason calls me and says, "Dude, you're not gonna believe this, but I just won two free tickets to the Smashing Pumpkins concert!" The concert was on Thursday night—the same night as the volleyball match.

To make a long story short, I went to the concert. I just couldn't pass it up. My parents fought me on it at first but then said, "You make up your own mind." If you want to know the truth, I only half enjoyed the concert. I got home late, and my sister was up, just sitting on the couch, looking sad. I said, "What's wrong, you get beat?" She just gave me a look and walked out of the room. That look hurt worse than if she'd hit me.

Corey, age 16

The urgent things in your life tug at your sleeves, shout, stamp their feet, whistle, do anything to get your attention, while the truly important things are in the background, waiting for *you* to come to them.

Corey realized too late that he didn't have his priorities straight in that situation. The concert seemed hugely important. But when the last note faded, he was back to the reality that he had let his sister down in something that was *truly* important.

Taking Action *Now*

Don't procrastinate. Procrastination comes from fear. It's like a protective fence for those who want to stay within their comfort zone. Procrastinators think, *If I don't do anything, no one will see my weaknesses or limitations. If I don't take part or take action, no one can judge me.* Procrastinators aren't people who don't know what to do; they're people who do know what to do, but for various reasons they don't take action. This attitude makes it extremely hard to reach goals.

By not acting when you know you should be doing something, you waste time. Procrastinate too much and life will pass you by. You will feel stuck. If you keep putting off looking into colleges, if you keep wondering how you would fare in a sport or a club or on a committee, if you keep putting off your studies to watch TV or talk with your friends, then remember this: Just like the person who sets his or her alarm, then shuts it off and oversleeps . . . *you snooze, you lose.*

It was like this little lightbulb going on over my head: Hey, you can play basketball as well as these guys who are on the team! I knew because I was playing pickup games with some of the better players and holding my own. But by then it was too late. It was in the middle of the season in my senior year. And I was really mad, because I knew I had been making excuses all these years. I kept thinking, "I'll get a little better and then go out next year." Well, "next year" never came.

Lawrence, age 18

Moving Toward Goals Daily

Do something daily that is truly important in moving you toward your goals. Invest your time in the important steps. When you take charge of your time, you take charge of your life. How you spend your time reflects your priorities. When you have trouble taking the steps to reach a goal, you need to ask yourself whether the goal really reflects your deepest needs, desires and values— your true priorities in life. When goals come from your deepest needs and values, it's not hard to go after them.

Four Keys to Staying Focused

You just read about four keys to staying focused on your vision. Complete this worksheet to see how well you're "in key" with your dreams and vision. Score yourself and see the scale at the end.

1. How often do you waste time on things you can't control?

Never	1
Seldom	2
Sometimes	3
Frequently	4
Always	5

2. How well are you able to let go of the past and focus on the present?

Extremely well	1
Very well	2
Okay	3
Not very well	4
Extremely poorly	5

3. How often are you distracted from truly important things by urgent things?

Never	1
Seldom	2
Sometimes	3
Frequently	4
Always	5

4. How often do you wish you could prioritize things better?

Never	1
Seldom	2
Sometimes	3
Frequently	4
Always	5

5. How often do you feel your decisions are based on your needs, beliefs, and values?

Always	1
Frequently	2
Sometimes	3
Seldom	4
Never	5

6. How often do you procrastinate on important tasks, decisions, or issues?

Never	1
Seldom	2
Sometimes	3
Frequently	4
Always	5

7. How often do you act—or not act—out of fear, only to wish later that you had acted differently?

Never	1
Seldom	2
Sometimes	3
Frequently	4
Always	5

8. How often do you take actions or steps toward your goals?

Always	1
Frequently	2
Sometimes	3
Seldom	4
Never	5

9. How much of your time is spent based on your priorities and what you want to achieve?

All of my time   1
Most of my time   2
Some of my time   3
Little of my time   4
None of my time   5

10. How well do you take charge of your time on a day-to-day basis?

Extremely well   1
Very well   2
Okay   3
Not very well   4
Extremely poorly   5

Score:

10–15: Excellent
16–20: Very good
21–25: Good
26–30: Okay
31–50: Poor

How did you score? If you didn't score so well, focus on those four keys to holding on to your dreams and vision.

Making Final Travel Plans

Once you have a plan for your journey with routes to specific stops along the way to your ultimate destination, it is important to check and see if you are packed properly. Are you fully prepared to begin the Success Process? Having a vision and goals and a plan to reach them is essential, but you have to make sure that you are properly prepared to begin your journey and to undertake it in a manner that is consistent with the principles and beliefs that you have chosen to guide your life.

When you are taking actions to reach your goals, always keep an eye on what is most important to you, so that in the process of going after your goals you don't get off track as a person. We all have heard of people who have achieved fame and fortune, only to have their lives fall apart because they neglected other important aspects. I know of a man who grew up in the Midwest, fought in Vietnam, and then came home and started off in business as a traveling salesman. Within a short time, he saw the opportunity to start his own business. He invited a friend to join him as a partner and together they built a multimillion-dollar manufacturing business. Without formal educations or any serious money in the bank, they created several businesses and profited beyond their wildest dreams.

But along the way, he lost his perspective. Making money and buying things became his total focus, to the extent that he neglected his relationships. He lives now in a mansion on his own estate, but in bitterness and hurt where there was once love and support. You can't buy those things. What a horrible feeling it would be to realize a dream and then to look at yourself and see that you have been so focused on where you were going that you lost sight of what you had become.

What if you achieved your goal to become a doctor, only to discover that you'd neglected your health so badly that you could no longer continue working? What if you fulfilled your vision of getting your master's degree, but had no one to share the victory with because in your march to that goal, you neglected your relationships, your friends and family? In the next chapter, I am going to offer you some "rules of the road" designed to help you stay on track and in touch as you journey through the Success Process.

5 Master the Rules of the Road

If there is no struggle, there is no progress.

Frederick Douglass

At this point you may be feeling pretty good about your journey along the Success Process: You've become more aware of who you are. You have a better sense of what you value and what you're competent in and capable of. You've at least begun to shape a vision for your life. And you've learned how to develop a plan to make that vision happen. Now you're ready to go, right?

Wrong. As I said in the last chapter, the road to success is a rocky one. Having a plan to negotiate that road is crucial, but there's a second part to being prepared for that rocky road: You need to have some tools handy to help you when things break down on the road (or to help *prevent* breakdowns), and you need to have some rules of the road to guide you along the way.

Tools and rules: That's what this chapter is all about. On these pages you'll learn about:

- Using determination to overcome obstacles and adversity,
- Letting your conscience be your guide,

- Using your willpower to keep on track,
- Tapping into your imagination,
- Leading a balanced, healthy life,
- Creating your own Rules of the Road, and
- Fulfilling responsibilities along the way.

Five tools and a set of rules: That's what you need to keep you going when the road gets rough and you appear to be going off course. We'll start with the tools first.

Identifying Your *Tools* for the Road

You can use any number of tools to help you both stay on track and make good progress on the road to success, but I'm going to focus on five:

- Determination
- Conscience
- Willpower
- Imagination
- Balance

If you can use these tools well, you can hang in there and eventually achieve your goals, no matter how difficult the road gets. Of the five tools, the most common among successful people—and thus perhaps the most important for you to develop and use—is determination.

Determination

Before we started dating, I used to water-ski quite a bit and I'd often told Oprah how much I enjoyed it. She said she would like to see me do it sometime, and the opportunity came on a trip to Florida. Now, I had talked my waterskiing talents way up, and I wanted to be able to dance, if not walk, on that water. The problem was, I didn't have my custom-made slalom ski with me. I had to have a special one because the standard ones don't fit my size-fifteen foot.

Without any choice, I squeezed into the slalom ski that was provided, but I had a great deal of difficulty getting up behind the ski boat because of the smaller ski. How much difficulty? I tried fifteen times and couldn't do it. I was out there on the water—make that *in* the water—for hours. The guy driving the boat told Oprah that he had never seen anyone so determined. Oprah told him: "If he doesn't get up he will keep trying until he dies, so you had better do whatever you can to get him up on those skis." She was right. I demanded that the boat driver keep trying. Meanwhile, Oprah was in the boat praying, "Oh Lord, please let him make it this time so we can go home!"

Even then, I didn't want to quit. But my arms became so sore they were actually swollen. I was really angry with myself for not making it up on the borrowed ski—so angry that I made everyone go back with me the next day to try again, and again, and again. It took twenty-three attempts before I finally made it up and water-skied. If I hadn't made it, we might still be out there.

My waterskiing story illustrates a very simple but important rule that I follow. If you want something in life you have to keep at it. Every time you fail, try again. If you fall down twenty-two times, go for twenty-three. You have to keep on keeping on when you are pursuing your dreams and goals. It is *always* too early to quit. That is an unspoken password for all successful people. As author Stephen Covey points out, the word "discipline" is derived from *disciple,* one who is devoted to something or someone. If you set goals and make plans you are on the right path, but if you aren't devoted to them, if you give up when the going gets tough or if you fall apart in the face of obstacles or opposition, you'll get nowhere.

> **I**t is *always* too early to quit.

"Everybody should have a dream," said Jesse Owens, the grandson of a slave and son of an Arkansas sharecropper. "Everybody should work toward that dream. And if you believe hard enough, whether it be in the Olympic Games, or in the business world, or the music world or the educational world, it all comes down to one thing. One day we can all stand on the top of the victory stand, and one day we can watch our flag rise above all others to the crescendo of our national anthem, and one day, you can say, on this day, 'I am a champion.'"

Jesse Owens began working in the cotton fields, picking a hundred pounds of cotton a day at the age of seven, so he knew a little bit about determination long before he became an Olympic athlete. He won four gold medals in the 1936 Olympics in Germany as Adolf Hitler watched and perhaps wondered how a black man from Arkansas could defeat his supposed "superior race."

Life responds to people like Jesse Owens, champions who never quit striving for their goals and dreams. And eventually, if you hang in there through the hard times and challenges, life will present you with opportunities to succeed. I'm reminded of a poster I saw recently. It had a photograph of a battered old rowboat stuck on a sandbar in the ocean. It was pretty forlorn-looking with its oars sticking up in the air. But the caption on the photograph was full of hope: THE TIDE ALWAYS TURNS.

It's true. If you hang in there and keep striving, most of the time the tide will turn. I have witnessed this in my life, and in the lives of many others, too. Perhaps the greatest example in modern times of the power of perseverance was the triumph of Nelson Mandela over apartheid in South Africa. Here was a man who had spent decades in prison because he dared to demand that his people be treated equally in their own nation.

I was blessed to personally meet and speak with this great man shortly after his release from prison after twenty-six years. I had met Mandela's family through a mutual friend who has business interests in South Africa. When it became known that Mandela was going to be freed, Oprah and I agreed to help his family members living in Boston return to their homeland once it was deemed safe. I accompanied Mandela's daughter, Zenani, and other family members on their return to their homeland. It was an experience I will never forget.

On February 11, 1990, hundreds of Africans had waited peacefully outside the gates of the Victor Verster Prison. A string of cars slowly came from within the prison grounds toward the gates. A silver sedan came right to the front entrance, stopped, and a slight, gray-haired man in a dark suit stepped out. I was watching then, from Chicago, thousands of miles away, but I had the same impression that would remain a few days later when I actually met him in person. I remember thinking that he seemed like such an unassuming, ordinary man, full of dignity and quiet but obvious strength. This was a lion who did not need to roar.

As Mandela spoke to the crowd on the day of his release, his delivery was very low-key. But his words were powerful. At first, he just looked into the sky, then he turned his gaze to the people in front of him and raised one clenched fist, then the other into the air. The crowd cheered but he did not speak to the crowd there. He got back into the car for a motorcade into Cape Town. The streets were lined with thousands of supporters. At one point, three traffic policemen requested his autograph, and Mandela gave it to them, signing their ticket books. It seemed like everyone in the world, black, white, or otherwise, was Mandela's friend that day.

Two days later in Soweto, more than 100,000 people had waited all day at the Grand Parade Stadium to hear his words as a freed man. What struck me was that after all those years of being imprisoned, taunted, and terrorized because of his dream for a free South Africa, Mandela was still fighting for what he believed in. He had won the respect of even his opponents, to the point that some were cheering and asking for his autograph that day. He called upon his followers to not let up their fight for freedom simply because he had been released. "Seize the moment," he told them, "so that the process towards democracy is rapid and uninterrupted. We have waited too long for our freedom. We can no longer wait. Now is the time to intensify the struggle on all fronts."

Mandela was well equipped for his journey. He possessed so much inner strength and determination that he made admirers of his jailers. Through the strength of his will, he forced the white power structure of South Africa to release him from prison. Even then, he kept on pursuing his dream of a free South Africa. Instead of retiring to a comfortable life, which he had surely earned, Mandela fought for free elections and for the top leadership position in the very nation that had tried to enslave him and his people.

My respect for him grew with every word I heard that day and it continued to expand during those days when I had the opportunity to observe him closely. I had breakfast and tea with Mandela and his family just a few days after his release. He had been conducting interviews with the media for days, but he seemed to draw strength from the air around him. He was so humble, very direct in what he had to say, and deeply principled. He was extremely grateful to us for bringing the family members back to him, and he was warm and loving to them.

Nelson Mandela's spirit proved so powerful that on election day in South Africa, he won the vote of even the grandson of the white leader who had been known as "the architect of apartheid." Mandela became the head of a nation that had imprisoned him, and on his inaugural day he proclaimed, "Let freedom reign." He proved that if you refuse to be broken, you cannot be enslaved. If there is any greater example of the power of determination, I do not know of it. It is extraordinary.

As Mandela showed us, life is a journey we travel one day at a time. Day by day and step by step, you have to maintain your vigilance and hold on to your vision for your life, no matter what happens around you or to you. To get where you want to go in life, you have to keep at it. You have to create a vision, make choices based on what moves you most swiftly toward your goals, and go after them with determination and single-mindedness. And whenever you encounter a problem, no matter how insurmountable it might seem, there is one simple response that should be ingrained in your behavior: Never give up.

Jesse Owens and Nelson Mandela became heroes around the world for their determination and triumphs, but every day people show remarkable courage and determination in their quiet struggles for better lives as well. I'll bet most folks have never heard of Jason Wessels of Galesburg, Illinois, but he went through a life-threatening and life-changing struggle that many of us would not have survived.

Jason was a basketball player on his high school team during the 1997–98 school year. In December 1997, he was struck down by a form of bacterial meningitis that eventually forced doctors to amputate both legs just below the knees to save his life. He also had all of his fingers amputated. For quite some time doctors were not optimistic that Jason would live. The community around him came to his support, but imagine going from being healthy and fit one moment to struggling the next moment, first to keep living and then to overcome the adversity of amputation. Jason, a senior when this happened, vowed from his hospital bed—even when doctors weren't sure that he would survive—to make it out of the hospital and to the Galesburg High School gym for Senior Night at the last home game. And, indeed, on Senior Night he was wheeled out on the floor by his mother, and he received a several-minute standing ovation. His mother graciously thanked the crowd for their ongoing support in the past few months, and there was hardly a dry eye in the house.

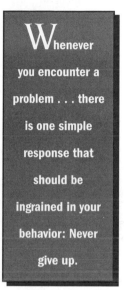

Whenever you encounter a problem . . . there is one simple response that should be ingrained in your behavior: Never give up.

Jason made his goal to be there that night in late February. It was the first time that he had been out of the hospital since he was admitted on Christmas night, the night he was struck by the meningitis. That same determination has helped him continue his education without looking back and bemoaning his fate. He is looking forward with the same dogged determination that helped him survive his crisis.

Jesse Owens, Nelson Mandela, and Jason Wessels never lost sight of what they were pursuing. They were determined and disciplined, and they persevered. Chances are you haven't been imprisoned for your beliefs, but certainly you have faced adversity of varying shapes and sizes. How have you responded? Do you wilt in the face of adversity and challenge, or do adverse circumstances energize you and motivate you to succeed? In the following worksheet, we'll help you to assess how determined an individual you are.

■ "Don't Tell Me I Can't Do It"

For some people, words to that effect are like premium-grade fuel for their engines—it's just what they need to get going. For others, hearing negative messages or facing obstacles makes them veer from their chosen path, even if that path is the right one for them. Answer the following ten True-False questions to see how you rate in your determination.

1. When people tell me I'm not capable of accomplishing something that is very important to me, I generally believe them and give up or alter my goals and shoot for something less than I really want.

True   False

2. When I come upon a roadblock and I don't know how to get around it on my own, I generally don't ask for outside help—from friends, parents, teachers, or mentors. I either need to figure it out on my own or just give up.

          True   **False**

3. When people doubt that I can do something so much that it feels like an attack on my self-worth, I stop focusing on my goal and spend my time trying to defend myself from the attack.

          True   **False**

4. I would rather be well-*liked* than well-*respected.* I'd prefer, of course, to be both liked and respected, but if I could only choose one, I'd choose to be liked.

          True   **False**

5. If the goals that come from my deepest values are not in line with those of my friends and peers, then I will change or drop those goals rather than lose my friends.

          True   **False**

6. In order not to hurt or upset my friends, I will compromise my deepest-held values and goals.

          True   **False**

7. In the face of adversity, I stand strong for my beliefs and values, unless I feel that the consequences (e.g., ridicule, loss of friends, disapproval from parents or teachers or coaches, etc.) are too great.

          True   **False**

8. Even when I believe strongly in something, I am often unable to overcome adversity, because I am afraid of failing. I would rather not try to overcome adversity than to risk failure.

          True   **False**

9. Roadblocks are signs that I am on the wrong road. People who are truly successful understand this and learn to "go with the flow" and get on a different road.

          True   **False**

10. When I come upon a roadblock, my first thought is to drop or change my plans, especially if the roadblock challenges me in new ways and forces me to step out of my "comfort zone."

True   False

Score

0–3   "False" answers: You are not very determined.

4–6   "False" answers: You are sometimes determined, but are often held back by adverse situations.

7–8   "False" answers: You are usually quite determined, but certain situations tend to hold you back.

9–10 "False" answers: You are extremely determined!

Don't be too upset if you scored low. You can develop determination as you grow. Life presents us with constant challenges through which we can grow and stretch our abilities to use determination to help us achieve our goals.

Now answer the following questions related to determination:

An example from my own life that best illustrates my determination to succeed in the face of adversity or obstacles is _____

_____

_____

_____

_____

_____

We all have gone through situations where, in hindsight, we wish we had stuck with our deeper values, but we were somehow swayed from doing so. Detail one time when you wish you had "stuck to your guns" but were swayed by friends or other influences to do something you didn't believe was right or that made you abandon or change a goal:

_____

_____

_____

_____

In retrospect, what could you have done differently in that situation? How could stronger determination have helped you?

_____

_____

_____

_____

If you had done things differently, as you've just described, how might the outcome have been different?

_____

_____

_____

_____

What types of feelings come to mind when you think of determined people? Awe? Respect? Inspiration?

_____

_____

_____

_____

What is one area in your life right now that could benefit from you being more determined?

_____

_____

_____

_____

What steps can you take to be more determined in that area?

_____

_____

_____

_____

Conscience

Your *conscience* is the inner voice that serves as a quality-control check on your actions. Your conscience says: *Is this what I should be doing? Why am I doing this?* It monitors your actions and attempts to keep them in line with your belief system.

Recently, there was a story in the newspapers about a Midwestern farmer whose son was nearly ripped apart in a farming accident; all of his limbs and most of his scalp were torn off, though one arm, both legs, and portions of the scalp were reattached. He was badly mangled, but somehow the boy survived. The family had no insurance, however, and the medical bills were more than $500,000. After media accounts of the family's crisis appeared around the country, nearly 100,000 people responded by sending donations to them.

The farmer accepted most of the donations, which were generally in the $5 to $25 range, but he turned down several in the $10,000 to $20,000 range because he felt it was too much to take. Once he saw that his son's medical bills were going to be paid, he began sending checks back to people, thanking them, but explaining that the family was now able to take care of itself. That farmer's con-

science was engaged. He was living out of his belief system rather than allowing himself to be seduced by greed or the power of material things.

Your conscience isn't engaged just in extreme situations such as that farmer's. Your conscience is there to guide you—if you allow it to—in everyday circumstances: whether or not to cheat on a test; to gossip and belittle people behind their backs; to use tobacco, alcohol, or other drugs. Oftentimes the things you are tempted to do or like to do are things that keep you from achieving goals and making your vision become reality. People who don't listen very well to their consciences are the type who later say, "I should have done such-and-such," or "I didn't think my doing such-and-such would result in *this.*" Or they say:

> I didn't plan to cheat on my history test. But a friend who had the test during first period gave me the answers. At first I got all nervous and was going to throw them away. But I didn't. I kept thinking about it all day, planning to toss the answers, but by the time sixth period rolled around . . . I hadn't thrown the answers away. I used them in class. I cheated and got an A. When I got my test back, I didn't feel good. I felt sick.
>
> Lynne, age 17

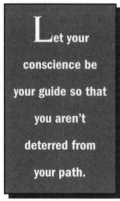

Let your conscience be your guide so that you aren't deterred from your path.

Let your conscience be your guide so that you aren't deterred from your path. Your conscience is one of the most useful tools you can use to keep you on target to reach your goals.

How do you develop your conscience and learn to tune into it effectively as you develop a plan to pursue your vision? Some people read the Bible, others turn to those around them whom they admire and respect. Keeping a daily journal can help you think about your feelings and experiences. A journal can help you engage your conscience in terms of whether you feel you've done right or wrong. Your conscience is all too easy to tune out in day-to-day living.

Of course, simply listening to your conscience isn't enough. You have to act upon that inner voice rather than following social trends or peer pressure. Following your conscience builds integrity, but it often takes willpower to do so.

Willpower

Your *will* gives you the power to respond to your conscience rather than to outside influences and distractions. The farmer might have been tempted to take all the money that was donated, but he had the will to act instead upon his conscience. You might feel compelled to talk about someone behind his or her back or to buy something you can't afford; but your conscience sounds the alert, and your will gives you the power to choose what is most compatible with your belief system.

Your will, then, helps you overcome your moods and fleeting desires to keep you on track for a life of integrity. You *can* say no to tobacco, alcohol, and other drugs. You *can* say no to gossiping and talking about others behind their backs. You *can* say no to taking part in activities that you know are wrong or that keep you from pursuing your goals. Your will keeps you going when the going gets tough, because it holds you to your long-term vision, blocking out short-term distractions.

You can add muscle to your willpower by working hard at keeping your promises, both those you make to yourself and those you make to others. Stephen Covey writes that if you want to learn to keep promises, you must first keep them to yourself. Every time you fail to do something that you said you would do, you reduce your value in the eyes of others.

"Jessica never does what she says she will do. Why believe her?" "LaVon will come through if it's easy enough. But if things get tough, then forget it. You never know about him." These kids are being branded—they are developing a reputation for not coming through. This is becoming their *brand name*—what they are known for. How you use your willpower will have a direct effect on what your brand name becomes.

Think about it. Coca-Cola is a brand. You expect a certain quality of taste with every can or bottle of Coke. Tide is a brand. You expect your laundry to come out fresh and clean every time you use Tide. You count on these products; they are known for their consistency and quality. That happens with people, too. You develop your own brand name for yourself. It's up to you how good a brand that is.

If you take promises seriously you won't promise much but you'll keep those promises. To work on your willpower, promise yourself you are going to lose five pounds and then do it. Promise yourself you are going to get half an hour of exercise every day of the week and then do it. Promise yourself you are going to get all your homework done and then do it. By living up to these small promises, you build strength to fulfill larger ones and you build confidence in your ability to control your own life rather than submitting to the control of others, or blaming outside influences for what happens in your life.

Imagination

Conscience is a rudder to guide you through choppy waters. Willpower is the inner strength to help you stay the course. And *imagination* is

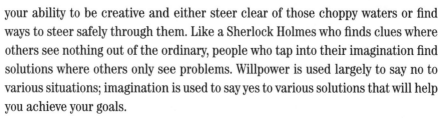

your ability to be creative and either steer clear of those choppy waters or find ways to steer safely through them. Like a Sherlock Holmes who finds clues where others see nothing out of the ordinary, people who tap into their imagination find solutions where others only see problems. Willpower is used largely to say no to various situations; imagination is used to say yes to various solutions that will help you achieve your goals.

Imagination is directly connected to vision. The greater your ability to imagine, the greater your ability to create a large and meaningful vision for yourself. People who use their imagination well tend to think "outside the box." They see things in different ways; they look at a problem from various angles and perspectives and aren't afraid to dream, to suppose, and to suggest alternatives.

The beginning of imagination is like brainstorming: There are no wrong answers, just a host of possibilities. Using your imagination means more than just being creative. It means being courageous, willing to take chances, willing to be open-minded, willing to pursue things in extraordinary ways. When you use your imagination, you greatly improve your chances to succeed, because you open up so many opportunities for yourself.

By using your imagination, you can learn to see yourself responding to problems, challenges, and bad situations in a more positive and productive man-

ner. And you can use your will to choose the best response over one driven by your emotions or moods. The best way to determine your own destiny is to create it and control it. This is a part of what true freedom is all about.

■ Conscience, Willpower, and Imagination: Three Powerful Tools for the Road

Starting off on your road to success without these three tools in tow is asking for trouble. Complete this worksheet to begin developing those tools for your journey.

You can use your conscience as a rudder to help guide you in making difficult decisions. How well do you usually listen to your conscience and use it in making tough decisions?

a. Not well at all.

b. I use it sometimes.

c. I use it quite often in making tough decisions.

In what types of decisions or situations do you find yourself most likely to act against your conscience?

_____

_____

_____

When you act against your conscience, what is a common outcome?

_____

_____

_____

What price do you pay for acting against your conscience?

_____

_____

_____

Name a situation when you were *tempted* to act against your conscience, but you listened to your conscience and were glad you did.

_____

_____

_____

Having a conscience would be quite frustrating if we didn't have willpower to *act* upon our consciences. What are the areas or situations in your life that call on your strongest willpower?

_____

_____

_____

Why do you need strong willpower in these areas or situations?

_____

_____

_____

Name a situation where you surprised yourself by acting on your conscience when you didn't think you had the willpower to do so.

_____

_____

_____

If you could have the willpower to change one attitude or habit, what would you change?

_____

_____

_____

You can use imagination as a bridge across dangerous waters. Name a time when you used your imagination to see an "escape route" or a path to take that no one else around you saw.

_____

_____

_____

Balance

In the previous chapter I talked about how all aspects of life are connected: Your schoolwork affects your personal life and social life; your family life affects your school life and social life; and so on. To be truly successful you need to lead a balanced life physically, socially, mentally, and spiritually. If you neglect one area, eventually the others will suffer.

Mental stress and anxiety, for example, can trigger physical illness. They can hurt your body as much as any virus by robbing you of sleep and proper digestion and weakening your body's resistance. Medical scientists now believe that stress can accelerate the spread of cancer; make you more vulnerable to viruses; and trigger asthma, ulcers, colitis, colds, and the flu. Being under stress is also thought to increase the risk of blocked arteries.

On the other hand, if one of the four aspects of your life is troubled, the others can be used to help it heal if they are strong. If you are knocked down by a physical ailment, you can call upon your spiritual beliefs, your faith, to help you get through the sickness. You can also call upon your mental strength and your social network of friends and family.

For me, personally, it helps to believe in God and to be able to turn to Him as a source of strength. My strong spiritual beliefs have gotten me through many hard times. Every day I say a prayer of thankfulness for the blessings bestowed upon me, and I also ask for guidance. Everyone has his or her own way of building strength; it is a very personal thing.

In developing your plan for acting on your goals, then, you need to understand that your physical, social, mental, and spiritual health are all connected. By tending to all of them, you can find a path to your goals that will keep you balanced, fulfilled, and happy in your journey. If you neglect any one of them, you run the risk of falling off the path, or going off in a direction that will not be as good for you. Now let's explore each aspect of health.

Physical Health

Your physical well-being is vital to your pursuit of a better life. Take care of your body by exercising, eating well, and getting adequate rest. If you don't do those things, you might hide your poor health for a while, but eventually your physical health will deteriorate and affect all parts of your life.

It is hard to concentrate on tasks when you're in poor physical health. Relationships can also suffer, and focusing on spiritual growth can be a challenge. When you work out every day, you build energy and a sense of empowerment. I work out nearly every day for several hours, playing tennis, racquetball, or basketball; lifting weights; and jogging, and I really look forward to it. If I miss even a day, I grow lethargic. I can feel my body weaken. Being physically healthy adds a great deal to every other aspect of your life.

If you have never been in great shape, it should become one of your priorities, a major goal. Exercise at a steady pace to get your heart rate up at least thirty minutes a day. Once you start, you will wonder how you ever let yourself slide. I promise you, it will change your life.

> I was never big into exercise, you know? I never played sports or anything, and I just felt too klutzy or embarrassed to do much. And I always just sort of felt "blah". . . not sick, but no energy, always tired, sort of sluggish.
>
> So I decided to try an aerobics class. I couldn't *believe* the difference it made! I felt better almost immediately. I have so much more energy now. You probably still couldn't drag me out to play basketball or softball—but if you're in my way and it's time for aerobics, look out!
>
> Jeanette, age 18

Social Health

Your social well-being focuses on your relationships. It's sad, but there are all sorts of toll-free numbers and Internet chat rooms available to people who are lonely and lacking real ties to other people. These are nothing more than modern lonely hearts clubs for people who have been unable, for whatever reasons, to make a connection and establish real relationships.

There is no substitute for real social interaction; all people need it. Nor is there any substitute for the qualities it takes to build relationships. You can fake charm, you can smile and be a smooth talker, but eventually you have to prove your integrity, your trustworthiness, and your sincerity. To live without love, trust, and mutual support is to live a hollow life. If you feel that your social health is not what it should be, I suggest that you take a step back and consider how others view relating to you. Are you trustworthy? Do you keep your word? Are you a good friend, someone who will *listen* as well as *talk?* Are you open with others? Are you a *giver* as well as a *taker* in relationships? Are you always talking about your own needs, wanting others to focus on those needs, but never willing to focus on others' needs?

Social health depends a lot on interpersonal and communication skills and maturity. There are many ways you can develop the social skills you need to lead a healthy social life. Work on being more trustworthy, on giving as well as taking, on being a good listener. Consider joining a club or special interest group that appeals to you. One of the best ways for shy people to meet others is to volunteer for charity work so that the focus is on helping others rather than on forced social interaction. You cannot deny the basic human need to interact with others.

> I always felt on the outside looking in. I don't know. If I was starting out in high school again I'd try to get better connected, to go out for a sport, join a club, do something. I never had that attachment. There were the jocks, the rich kids, the brains and geeks, the druggies. I didn't really fit in anywhere. It made my life pretty hard, I can tell you.
>
> Clint, age 19

Mental Health

You fuel your mental well-being by being positive and optimistic. You maintain it through continual learning and growth. The next time you go to a class reunion, a large family reunion, or any big gathering of people, look to see where most of the energy is focused. Generally, it is upon those people who are successful and positive. The people with the opposite form of energy, the negative, pessimistic types, will generally be found off in their own corner, or sitting alone. If you listen, you'll hear them grumbling about how life has done them wrong.

People who are actively engaged in the Success Process are hungry for knowledge and aware of what is going on in the world around them. They read books, magazines, and newspapers to stay on top of the issues of the day. They ask questions more often than they offer answers. They form their opinions based on as much information as they can gather rather than on pure emotion or knee-jerk reaction.

Obviously, you cannot pursue a better life without being in good mental health with an alert mind. For a time, it was considered a cliché to urge people to *be optimistic* in their mental approach, but that has changed. Increasingly, researchers are finding that an optimistic attitude is every bit as important as a high IQ in predicting an individual's ability to achieve his or her goals and dreams.

These researchers have found that people with a pessimistic approach to life tend to believe that bad things are inevitable, that they somehow triggered them, and that the problem will last a long time, undermining all of their plans. This negative attitude feeds on itself and fosters depression. Pessimists focus on the problems that they feel they face.

A person with an optimistic mental attitude, on the other hand, tends to view bad times as temporary, failure as a step to eventual success, and misfortune as the result of circumstances beyond his or her control. Optimists focus on solutions that they feel await their discovery.

If you feel your mental health is hindered by pessimism, I'd suggest you break the habit first by focusing on a solution. There are many books now that offer advice on how to train yourself to be more optimistic in your approach to life. It might also help to develop relationships with positive, optimistic people.

> An optimistic attitude is every bit as important as a high IQ in predicting an individual's ability to achieve his or her goals and dreams.

I guess I never saw the point in trying so hard, in torturing myself to get decent grades, because I figured it would never happen. I mean, I could spend all semester sweating over my geometry book and be lucky to get a C. And if I worked *really* hard, I'd get what? A C+? What's the point?

I remember this kid, Gerald. Everybody made fun of him 'cause he was sort of dumb. But he never seemed to mind. He took it all in stride and did his thing and just generally got along with everyone. Nobody made fun of him *too* bad, 'cause he was so sweet. He always saw the good in people and I guess in himself too.

So Gerald, he was in my geometry class. He didn't know that stuff any better than he knew pig latin. But he'd just keep at it, he'd study all the time, he'd ask questions in class and everyone would laugh, but he didn't care. He wanted to learn. And then it sort of dawned on me: He was gonna learn the stuff, because he just kept telling himself he could do it! And I thought, man, if he can do it, I can do it.

This ain't no fairy tale. Gerald got a C–. He was lucky to get that. But he got it, and he was happy with it. If he'd had my attitude, he'd've flunked for sure.

First semester I got a C–, just like Gerald. But the dude inspired me. It nearly cracks me up to say it, but I began to think like Gerald. And I got a B next time around.

Denzel, age 16

105

Spiritual Health

Your spiritual well-being begins with how you feel about yourself but it does not end there. It runs much deeper into the realm of how you relate to others, respond to others, and what you bring into the lives of others. Having a solid spiritual base promotes self-discipline, an inner calm, and an ability to love others as much as you love yourself—all of which are essential tools for your journey to a better life.

Understand, though, that your life has a spiritual quality only when it is based on something other than self. Animals live for themselves. Humans, hopefully, live to serve something greater than the individual. Organized religion is a primary method to build spiritual health, but there are many others ways, including the study of ancient philosophies. Some people build spiritual health by reading Scripture; some by meditating in a darkened room; some by sitting on the beach basking in nature's beauty; some by listening to beautiful music, reading powerful literature, or looking at great works of art.

There are those who act as though this aspect of human existence has no connection to their lives. True, it is possible to achieve your goals without having a healthy spiritual life. Whether or not you can fully appreciate and enjoy those successes without a spiritual base is another matter.

> I try to keep things in perspective. My friends say, "How can you be so calm all the time? Aren't you alive?" They like to give me a hard time. Well, things do bother me, I get upset or ticked off at someone, but it passes and I realize there are bigger things, spiritual things, things that maybe don't give you the answer for everything but give you a peace about it. If I didn't have a good spiritual life, a base, my life would be a mess, let me tell you!
>
> Cassandra, age 17

■ Leading a Balanced, Healthy Life

The road to success is best traveled when the physical, social, mental, and spiritual aspects of your life are all healthy and in balance with each other. Complete this worksheet on those four aspects to see how balanced your life is.

What do you do now to lead a healthy physical life?

_____

_____

_____

What steps could you take to improve your physical health?

_____

_____

_____

What do you do now to lead a healthy social life?

_____

_____

_____

What steps could you take to improve your social life?

_____

_____

_____

What do you do now to lead a healthy mental life?

_____

_____

_____

What steps could you take to improve your mental health?

_____

_____

_____

What do you do now to lead a healthy spiritual life?

_____

_____

_____

What steps could you take to improve your spiritual health?

_____

_____

_____

Determining Your Rules of the Road

You've learned about the *tools* that you need for the road to success: determination, conscience, willpower, imagination, and balance. Now you'll learn about the *rules* of the road that can help guide you along the way.

When you receive your driver's license or when you take the test for license renewal, you are given a guidebook—the rules of the road. It contains the traffic laws for your state and identifies road signs. I want you to create your own Rules of the Road that establish guidelines for how you will travel along the Success Process.

Base these rules on the values and principles that you have chosen to guide your life. They should help you stay on course to your goals and give you the strength and determination to fight and overcome distractions, hardships, and obstacles. I am sure you know that Jesse Owens, Nelson Mandela, and Jason Wessels were all sorely tested in their pursuit of better lives. Owens was taunted by armed Nazis. Mandela was beaten and placed in a former leper colony. Wessels had his legs and fingers amputated.

How did they persevere? How did they stay focused? How did they not lose their way? At one point during his imprisonment, Mandela was offered a deal by his jailers. If he would renounce his call for majority rule and go quietly into retirement, he could go free. He had already made his point, his jailers argued. No one would blame an old man for wanting to go home. But he refused. He said he would rather stay in jail than sell out his principles.

Mandela had very well-defined rules for the road. Most of us, whether consciously or unconsciously, live our lives within guidelines or principles that have stood the test of time, concepts as simple but as lasting as the Golden Rule: *Do unto others as you would have them do unto you.*

Your personal Rules of the Road are guidelines for a life of quality and integrity. If you stand by them, you are more likely to be successful in *all* aspects of your life—physical, social, mental, and spiritual. I'd like you to come up with five Rules of the Road that guide your life, but first I'll offer a list of my own as an example. Mine are simple, but they are based on time-tested principles.

1. *Be honest.*

    As someone who always tries to build value in his life, I believe that you have no value to other people if they can't believe what you say. Trust is built on perceptions of honesty. Throughout my life I have known people whom I have enjoyed being with but whom I did not fully trust and so the relationships did not go very far. None of us are perfect. Even when our intentions are good, sometimes we can't always do what we say we are going to do. But if you are honest with people even when you fail, you at least maintain your credibility over time.

2. *Do the work that is required.*

    What you put into any project, plan, or endeavor is reflected in how it turns out. Why waste your time doing something halfheartedly? I'm guilty sometimes of spreading myself too thin, but I have come to realize that it is far more satisfying to take on fewer tasks and concentrate on doing them well.

    You know in your heart what you need to do to realize your goals. If you do less, it only hurts you. An Olympic runner might want to cut a couple of miles off his training route each day, but he knows that doing so will hurt his performance. Don't make excuses. Do the work that is required.

3. *Maintain a positive attitude.*

    Being positive begins with eliminating the negative. That includes negative thoughts in your mind, negative relationships, anything that interferes with your ability to move forward. Recently one of my family members called my administrative assistant about a family reunion that I was hosting and made threats. This family member has abused our relationship in the past. I was tempted to call this person back and let him have it, but I decided to leave that negative energy untapped. Sometimes the best way to take the power away from a negative person is to just ignore him or her.

4. *Take the time to think things through.*

    We have a wonderful capacity to think, but too often we submit to the temptation to act without giving enough thought beforehand. So much of what we do is to *react* because immediate action gives more instant gratification; but if you develop a pattern of thinking about what you are doing first, you eliminate many errors and crises. Those who take time to think and plan out their lives are the ones who get the greatest benefit out of whatever they are involved in.

5. *Look at the big picture.*

    Too many people think first from the point of "me." That is small-picture thinking. If you look at the big picture, your thought processes revolve around how you can make a difference in the lives of others. Looking at the big picture also gives you perspective on how your actions and words will affect those around you. When you operate from this perspective, you offer leadership to those around you, and being a leader creates greater opportunities for you.

■ Creating Your Own Rules of the Road

In the space below, write your own Rules of the Road to help guide the way you live. Review them often so that you stay on track.

1. _____

_____

2. _____

_____

3. _____

_____

4. _____

_____

5. _____

_____

Using Your Rules of the Road

Refer to your Rules of the Road as you take action on your goals. Check them if you feel your life has lost balance. Keep in mind also that while you should be goal-oriented, it is important not to lose sight of the things you value in life. Remember the key questions: What kind of person do you want to be ten years from now? Twenty years from now? At the end of your life? What will people say about you when you are gone? I think Stephen Covey would have to agree, when you consider those thoughts you are certainly beginning with the *real end* in mind.

How can you use your Rules of the Road in day-to-day living? Say that tomorrow you go to school and:

- The deadline on your American Lit project just got moved up one week.
- Your project partner just moved and you have to do the project alone.

- You receive huge assignments in three other classes.
- You are coming up on your busiest time of the year for your participation in sports or another extracurricular activity.

Now, you might easily be tempted to follow the standard practices of prioritizing, postponing, ignoring, rearranging, and dodging. All are time-honored methods of crisis management. But where do they get you?

Instead, by stepping back and viewing the demands on your time from a deeper perspective, you may be able to deal with solutions rather than the problems. Here's how I would apply my Rules of the Road to this situation:

1. *Be honest.* First, I'd be honest with myself: Can I do the work in the time allotted? This isn't a chance to give myself an out on the project; it's a time to honestly evaluate what I can do. If I feel I can accomplish all the tasks in the time given, fine. If not, I'll talk to my American Lit teacher and explain the situation. Because my project partner moved, I may be given some leeway.

2. *Do the work that is required.* My goal isn't to get *out* of work; it's to do the work required, and to do it well. I may need more time to do it, given special circumstances such as I've described, but I still want to complete all the projects. What I'd like to do is have a reasonable amount of time to complete the projects well.

3. *Maintain a positive attitude.* No matter what the schedule, I'm going to do better in my work if I have a positive attitude. Even if I'm not granted any extension on a project, I'll do better on the portion that I can complete if I maintain a positive attitude. And I'll be much more likely to accomplish more than I thought I could if I remain positive.

4. *Take the time to think things through.* If my American Lit teacher won't allow an extension on the due date, maybe she'll allow me to turn it in with everyone else but then continue to work on it for another week. Or maybe one of my other teachers will allow an extension on a project. Or maybe I could cut back on my extracurricular activity for a week. Or maybe, for one week, I could grit my teeth and get up one or two hours early to work on my projects. Or I could not hang out with my friends or watch TV for a week to gain time to work.

5. *Look at the big picture.* This rule doesn't directly apply as I've written it. But another way of looking at the big picture is this: How will this experience affect me? Will I learn from it, grow from it? Will I keep it in perspective? What will I gain from it to make me a better person? How will I interact with my teachers and my coach or club coordinator? How will my

handling of this situation affect those around me—my teachers, fellow students, friends, family?

Not all of your rules will apply to every situation, of course. Sometimes only one or two might apply, but that will be enough to guide you.

The key is to stop focusing on problems and start focusing on solutions. You can apply this approach in family matters, too. When my daughter was considering which college to attend and what to major in, we sat down together and instead of approaching it by considering the problems of location, costs, admission policies, and so on, we focused on what her goals were for her life. I asked her *"What do you want to be doing in ten years?"* And from that wider and deeper perspective, we worked together to find a college and determine a course of study that would get her where she wanted to be in ten years.

When you keep your goals and your vision for your life in alignment with your rules for living, you don't get easily thrown off. When you are *living large* you don't allow yourself to get beaten down and swept under by a system or the daily grind. You find ways to change that system and to transform the grind into a game you can win. You tend to view all of life as a success process; you don't get easily frustrated or angry.

> When you are living large you don't allow yourself to get beaten down and swept under by a system or the daily grind.

You tend to see problems as opportunities to exercise your talents and knowledge. You aren't afraid of challenges because you know they stimulate growth, just as lifting weights builds strength. This also helps you to see differences in opinion with other people as natural and expected and valuable because those differences challenge you to understand and seek common ground.

Fulfilling Responsibilities Along the Way

There is one last thing to consider before setting off on your journey. You can't leave your responsibilities at home. It is vital that you consider how your actions along the way will affect all aspects of your life, on every relationship and responsibility that you have. Many of life's conflicts come when we focus on one aspect of life but neglect another, when we work so hard at our schoolwork or jobs or are so busy with extracurricular activities that we neglect our relationships.

Each of us has many roles to fill. I am an employer, a board member, a partner in a relationship, a father, a son, a friend, a club member, among other roles. When I put together a plan for achieving my goals, I had to consider what impact my actions would have on each of those roles and how I could balance them all while pursuing my vision.

In the next worksheet, you'll consider the roles you play and your long-term goals within those roles so that you can fulfill your responsibilities while fulfilling your vision.

■ Roles and Goals

Consider all of your relationships, affiliations, and duties and then write down the roles that you fill. For instance, you might be a student, a son, a friend, and a band member; or a student, a daughter, a sister, a friend, and an athlete.

Role 1 _____

Role 2 _____

Role 3 _____

Role 4 _____

Role 5 _____

Do you neglect some roles because you dwell too much on the others? Which role seems most neglected?

_____

Are all the roles in harmony with your vision for your life? If not, should you consider eliminating some roles? (For instance, if you listed "boyfriend" or "girl-friend," but you feel that you are neglecting your role there, perhaps it's because your day is so filled by trying to fulfill your other roles that you don't have the time to give to the relationship that it deserves.)

_____

_____

Review your roles and determine what is most important. List those roles again and write down your long-term goal for each role.

Example: In my role as a student, I will take the classes that will best prepare me for college. I will take classes in my areas of interest and take leadership roles in those classes, because I know the more I put into a class, the more I get out of it.

Role 1 _____

  Goal _____

_____

Role 2 _____

  Goal _____

Role 3 _____

  Goal _____

_____

Role 4 _____

  Goal _____

_____

Role 5 _____

  Goal _____

_____

To properly serve each of your roles in life, you have to use the five tools I've talked about—determination, conscience, willpower, imagination, and balance. And you have to apply your own Rules of the Road to keep you on track in each role. Balance is especially critical here; life is a process of continually seeking balance. The key to achieving balance is in realizing that your roles are all interrelated. Understand that even though your life will naturally run in cycles that place the focus on one role over another from time to time, over the long run, balance is essential.

At the beginning of the chapter I tried to slow down those of you who were ready to barge out the door and embark on your journey without having the five tools to use along the way, and without having any Rules of the Road to use as guideposts. Now we're ready to embark. The next chapter addresses those who would prefer to stay at home, to stay in their comfort zones. In the next chapter we'll talk about stepping outside the box, venturing into personally uncharted territory. Creating and fulfilling a vision necessarily means going places you haven't gone before.

6 Step into the Outer Limits

Some of us are timid. We think we have something to lose so we don't try for the next hill.

Maya Angelou

In the last two chapters I've talked about developing a travel plan and mastering the Rules of the Road. Now we're going to begin to put that plan and those rules to use. You don't need much of a plan or too many rules if you're just going down the road a few miles, on a path you've traveled a thousand times and could do (and maybe have done) nearly in your sleep. Plans and rules are most effective and useful when coupled with a journey that takes you into *uncharted territory.*

I'm going to challenge you to go perhaps not "where no man has gone before," but where *you* have not gone before. Living a successful life is necessarily filled with expanding your horizons, testing yourself, stretching yourself, and challenging yourself. After all, a vision isn't much of a vision if all it encompasses is what you've done before. Life is about *growth.*

When I was a boy, I watched some of the scariest shows on television: *Alfred Hitchcock Presents, The Twilight Zone,* and, maybe the scariest for me, *The Outer Limits.* I don't know why I watched those shows because I'd have trouble getting to sleep after sitting through them with my hands over my eyes. For me,

The Outer Limits was the scariest because of the way it always began with the image on the television screen flickering and then turning into static and this scary voice saying that control of your television set had been taken over for the next sixty minutes.

Loss of control is a scary thing for most people. No one likes the thought of losing control, even when, in truth, the person may not really be in control in the first place. It is natural for people to want to stay with what is familiar and comfortable in their lives rather than for them to venture into the unknown. Most people want to stay within their *comfort zones,* where they feel safe and secure.

Fear of the unknown is one of the greatest obstacles that you will face in life. But if you want a better life, you must learn to overcome that natural fear and step outside what has become comfortable and familiar. You must risk losing control in order to push yourself into the outer limits of your abilities and talents. That is how you move to a higher level of achievement. It is the way to a better life.

In this chapter we'll focus on the importance of extending yourself. You'll learn how you can

- Push yourself to your own outer limits,
- Take calculated risks,
- Learn from failure and criticism, and
- Take control of your life.

Without your ability to do these things, your engine may be finely tuned, but it's in neutral. Once you learn how to step into the outer limits, you're ready to shift into gear and move forward. You are, in effect, engaging your vision and your plans with a drive that will take you places you've never been before.

Extending Your Limits

You have numerous opportunities to extend yourself, go where you've never gone before, and grow through the experience. One way to look at it is to consider your life as a circle with opportunities for growth all around the outside of that circle. There is no single door through which you must walk to push through to the "other side"; you can stretch yourself and grow—in effect, go outside your circle—from anyplace within. All around that circle you could label the things that are important to you—family, friends, education, personal development, specific goals and aspirations, and so on. And in each area you could take steps beyond the familiar, into uncharted territory and new growth. People who are successful are forever expanding their circles. This is a lifelong process.

If you want to be successful in this process, you must be willing to do two things: leave your comfort zone and use all your talent. We'll look at those two aspects next.

Leaving Your Comfort Zone

Take a minute now to look at your life. Are you stuck in a comfort zone in any aspect? Here's one student who is:

I'm not going to college. No one else in my family has; why should I? I've worked at Kellerman's [a gas station] for the last two summers, and Mr. Kellerman says I can work there full time after I graduate. I mean, I know cars, and the work's okay. It's a job. What else am I supposed to do?

Josh, age 17

If the work's only "okay" at age seventeen, what's it going to be like at twenty-seven and thirty-seven? I've known people who have stayed in dead-end jobs that drained the life out of them because they preferred the security of a no-brainer job to the challenge of a potentially more energizing one.

When your comfort zone isn't even truly comfortable but you stay in it because you would rather deal with the *known* than the *unknown,* your life is being guided by fear rather than hope. That is no way to live. In fact, you are not really living when your fears control your actions. Instead, you are hiding from life.

As you proceed on your journey in pursuit of a better life, you may begin to feel uncomfortable because you are entering new territory. Pursuing your dreams requires you to leave your comfort zone and to push into areas where you at first have less control. When you set out on your journey, you have to be willing to grow, to push your talents to the outer limits. That means pushing beyond what is known to you, taking risks, and learning to view failure as merely a step, rather than a defeat, in your journey along the Success Process.

To live a fulfilling life, you can't always cling to what is comfortable, not if you want to keep growing and bettering yourself. I'm not a kid anymore, but my comfort zone is still in sports. Although I haven't played professional basketball for more than twenty-five years, I still am more at home playing sports than anywhere else. I still love the competition, the exhilaration of physical exercise, and the camaraderie of sports. I have to admit, it feels great when I hear someone say, "Stedman can still play the game." Sports are definitely within my comfort zone. But it wasn't until I stepped out of the comfort of my athletic career that I saw the greater possibilities for my life. I could have continued to play basketball in Europe for many years, but I knew that playing professional basketball was not something I could do forever. I was eager to grow.

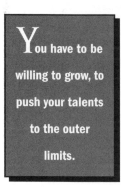

You have to be willing to grow, to push your talents to the outer limits.

We all have our comfort zones. They aren't, in and of themselves, bad things. They simply are indicators of what areas of our lives we feel most safe and secure in. The goal is not to go toward a life of feeling unsafe and insecure. Rather, it's to continually stretch those comfort zones, which necessarily means stepping outside them to experience the unknown, and make the unknown known, to, in essence, feel more and more comfortable with bigger and better things.

A comfort zone is simply a marker indicating, "Beyond this point I am going to be challenged. The outcome beyond this point is not known, and I take risks going beyond." It's true; there are risks involved in leaving your comfort zone (or, put another way, in working to expand your comfort zone). If you don't leave your comfort zone, however, you may miss out on the best opportunities for using all your talent.

Using *All* Your Talent

You should regularly assess your position in life, asking yourself whether you are moving forward, standing still, or even going backward in the Success Process. Again, this process does not necessarily refer to financial or career success but to living a fully engaged life in which all of your gifts and talents are developed and put to their highest use.

Successful people are experts at using their gifts and talents. Money is a by-product of success, but it is not necessarily an indicator of it. Plenty of wealthy people are not truly successful, in the largest sense, and plenty of people who are not wealthy are living very successful and fulfilling lives. The key is to what extent you are using your talents and gifts.

It's easy to get comfortable at one level of achievement and then just kick back and coast. Then, before you know what hit you, you find yourself *stuck*. One morning you wake up, look around, and ask yourself, "What happened to my dream for my life? What about all those great things I was going to accomplish? All the adventures and dreams I had envisioned for my life? How did I get stuck?"

You get stuck by forgetting that life is a process of continual striving and challenge, of pushing your talents and knowledge. Sounds like work, doesn't it? That's why so many people get stuck. And it's not just people undergoing "midlife crises" who feel stuck. It's young adults, not much older than yourself. It's people who work in dead-end jobs or who are in bad relationships or who get tangled up in a life of drugs and crime. It's people who have no idea what they want out of life and then blame life or other people for their troubles. It's people who live down to their low expectations for themselves and who suffer in silence, not wanting to draw attention to themselves. It's people who make bad choices early on in life and then don't know how to choose something better.

What about you? Do you get up in the morning *excited* about the potential for the day? Do you have a vision for your future and are you taking steps to attain that vision? Or are you just coasting, no plan, no destination in mind, no clue as to what you can do today to build toward a better tomorrow, skirting every challenge that comes your way? At the end of your life, will you look back and say, "I used life up! I rode it all the way, I took all of my talents and abilities as far as they would go"? Or will you say, "I stopped too soon. I sold myself short. I could have done better, I could have done more. I settled for the consolation prize instead of the grand prize"?

That's not to say that you can't find happiness somewhere other than the destination that you had originally set out for. It happens all the time. Life doesn't follow a set script. Take, for example, the movie *Doc Hollywood.* In it, a young doctor, played by Michael J. Fox, sets out for California to be a plastic surgeon, but en route he gets delayed in a small southern town and eventually, in spite of himself, finds love and fulfillment there. He tries to stick with his original dream, but when he checks his beliefs, values, and principles, he discovers that the small-town family practice and the woman he has fallen in love with are much more in line with what he really values. That is why it is important to always use your values and principles as guidelines when you travel in the Success Process. If you are feeling stuck, odds are that what you are doing is not in line with your values and your expectations for your life.

> At the end of your life, will you look back and say, "I used life up! I rode it all the way, I took all of my talents and abilities as far as they would go"?

Oh yeah, well I've settled for a pretty nice life, you might say. If you are content with your life, fine, but don't *settle* for anything. Don't compromise your goals and dreams. When you live life to the fullest, you don't *settle* for anything. You use up all your energy. And at the end, you check out of this world with all your gauges on empty, every talent and ability and interest exhausted.

There are people in my hometown, people my age, who were afraid to leave the security of their lives there. I'm sure you know similar people. You go home and run into them, and they have no more energy than the sidewalk. That's not to say that there are not people who stay in their hometowns and lead very good, meaningful, and fulfilling lives. Many people do; they find ways to energize their lives, and because of them, their communities continue to thrive.

But others stay where they grew up because they are afraid to venture outside the comfortable and familiar and they don't seek new ways to use their talents and gifts. They never take life on. Again, you don't necessarily have to change locations to do that. You can change the world with an idea even if you never leave your front porch. The late Sam Walton, the founder of Wal-Mart, never left Arkansas, yet he certainly had a powerful impact. The Success Process is really an inner journey and it requires courage to take the risks along the way, and to truly use all your talents as you go.

■ Extending Boundaries, Expending Talents

To live to your full potential, you will always face risks; growth requires you to leave your comfort zone. Leaving a comfort zone takes courage. This worksheet will help you explore your comfort zone, as well as ways to get the most out of your talents.

Consider one of the important areas of your life: relationships; education; personal development; or individual pursuits such as music, the arts, or sports. Consider an area in which you feel competent, yet somewhat stagnant; you haven't experienced too much growth in the last year or so in this area. You have, in effect, established your "comfort zone" in it and haven't pushed beyond, even though you may be experiencing a certain level of success in it. But you feel, deep down, that you can do *more*. When you stop to really think about it, you get frustrated, because you're just doing the "same old same old." Now answer these questions:

What is your comfort zone? In whatever particular area of your life you have chosen to examine here, what are you comfortable in doing or accomplishing?

_____

_____

_____

What potential action or growth makes you begin to feel *uncomfortable*?

_____

_____

_____

Why do you think that makes you feel uncomfortable?

_____

_____

_____

What would you *really* like to achieve in this area?

_____

_____

_____

What holds you back from achieving this, and why does it (or why do these things) hold you back?

_____

_____

_____

If you took steps beyond your comfort zone, what might happen?

_____

_____

_____

In chapter 3 you explored your talents and ways you could envision using your talents. The goal is to not just know what your talents are, but to *use* them. Now take the time to dream a little dream—in fact, two dreams.

Dream 1: Describe an "easy way" to use your talents in a career after you're finished with your education and are making your own way in the world. This way is the most obvious way and although it would call on your talents, it wouldn't necessarily stretch you or help you use those talents to the fullest. This way is a little-risk way; the path is pretty clear and the outcome is pretty well known.

_____

_____

_____

Dream 2: Now describe a way in which you might use your talents that would truly challenge you—a way that involves risk, and that energizes you to meet the challenges you would face. This way would be exciting, perhaps sometimes unnerving, but ultimately many times more rewarding than the "easy way" described in Dream 1.

_____

_____

_____

Which dream do you want to follow?

_____

Taking Risks

Just as a tree grows by pushing buds up through the existing branches, you have to push yourself to grow beyond your current circumstances. This is where you have to walk the walk if you are serious about changing your life. It takes courage to take risks, to do things that you feel may expose you to the possibility of danger, loss, or failure.

Because of the potential for those negative outcomes, most people—other than stuntmen and daredevils—avoid taking risks as much as possible. But can you really escape taking risks in life? What can you do that has no risk to it? Love your family? Coast through school, taking the easiest classes and not getting involved in clubs and extracurricular activities that are in your areas of interest? Go along with the crowd for fear of being singled out as different?

The truth is that nothing is risk free. Loving your family members involves the risk of losing them, or having them hurt you with their behavior, but no one would consider withholding love rather than taking that risk. Any relationship involves risk, but if you spend your whole life avoiding involvement because you don't want to get hurt, what sort of life will you have? A lonely one.

Coasting through school and through life brings with it the risk of boredom and of dissatisfaction with life or, rather, with your *response* to life. There are few things as draining and depressing as taking the safe and easy way out, and knowing that in doing so you are merely coasting. Coasting may be easy, but it's far from exhilarating and fulfilling.

Going along with the crowd can be rife with risks, depending on the crowd you run with. It might be the easiest solution for the moment, but if you "go with the flow" and follow the crowd, you might be following it down a path that leads to trouble with your parents or the law, to getting low grades or getting kicked out of school and having limited job opportunities later in life, to debasing

123

your body with tobacco and drugs, and so on. "The crowd" is *not* a good barometer for the risks you should encounter and the decisions you should make.

> Stephon told me, "This is a test for you. You want to be one of us, you deliver the bag." I said I didn't want to deliver no bag. At first there was no way I was gonna do it. But we had this "discussion." And I just felt myself giving in, against my will. I said, "Man, what if I get caught?" Stephon smiled and said, "If you one of us, you don't *get* caught. That's the test." I didn't have nothing else, nobody else to look to. This was it for me. I knew it was wrong. But I didn't see any way out. I wanted to hang with these guys, you know?
>
> So I took the bag and I got caught. Now I got a record. I've gone back to that day a thousand times, wishing I could change it. It was the dumbest thing I've ever done.
>
> Antoine, age 19

In reality, you are always taking risks. Sometimes doing nothing about your situation is itself a risk. Risk is like a coin with two sides. On one there is the possibility of failure; on the other is the opportunity for gain. Remember this about risks: *If you continue to do what you have always done, you will continue to get the same result you have always gotten. But if you take well-calculated risks, you can make great progress.*

Focus, then, not on whether you should take risks, but on what risks you should take, how you should take them, and what attributes you need to be an effective risk-taker. Here are some of those attributes:

1. To be a risk taker, you need courage and mental and moral strength to take on your fears.

   That strength comes from a clear vision of what you want for your life and from a focus on your deepest values, needs, and desires. A clear vision and strong focus give you the power to pursue your goals in spite of fears and challenges.

   Anthony Watson often thinks of the fears that nearly overwhelmed him as a boy growing up in Chicago's Cabrini-Green neighborhood, which is widely known today as one of the most violent in the country. In his childhood, it was not nearly as overrun with gangs and crime, but it was still a tough place. He often wondered whether he would grow up to take a place among the winos who populated a street corner near his family's apartment. He avoided alleys and even certain streets, where people he had known had lost their lives, and he paid protection dues to neighborhood bullies, giving them fifty cents to let him live another five minutes, or so they'd threaten.

Fears dominated his school days, too. On his first day in the sixth grade at Cooley Upper Grade Center, an older boy spit on him. Yet with the help of his parents, John and Virginia, Anthony faced his fears and overcame them. He became a good student and a standout football player, building confidence and courage that served him well after he earned an appointment to the United States Naval Academy in Annapolis, Maryland. But there, too, Anthony had to overcome hostility and his own fears as one of only a handful of urban blacks. He did it, reaching deep within for courage and strength, and he won over even classmates who had predicted he would never make it. In fact, they elected him president of their freshman class by a 98 percent majority.

Now a veteran naval officer, there is little doubt that Anthony Watson will still have to face hostility and challenges in his life. That is to be expected, particularly when you are the commander of a nuclear-powered submarine. But there is no doubt that Commander Watson will be up to the challenges that await him.

> If you continue to do what you have always done, you will continue to get the same result you have always gotten. But if you take well-calculated risks, you can make great progress.

2. As a risk taker, you must believe in your ability to overcome obstacles and to solve problems.

A *can do* attitude is essential for taking risks. When you have this attitude, you understand that failure is not the end of the road. You realize that through failure you can learn how to succeed and grow. The lessons you learn from things that don't work help you to discover those things that do work.

It's been said that Thomas Edison had hundreds of failures before he finally came up with a lightbulb that worked. Yet Edison didn't view those failures as defeats. He viewed them as steps in the process of success. "Results!" he once said, "why, man, I have gotten a lot of results. I know several thousand things that won't work."

As a scientist, Edison understood that even failed experiments offered information that could eventually lead to success, but only if he kept working and trying and constantly evaluated his progress. "Many of life's failures are people who did not realize how close they were to success when they gave up," he said.

3. As a risk taker, you must be willing to experience failure.

It is up to you to decide whether those failures will become defeats or whether they will lead to successes. When you learn to take risks and to view failure as part of the Success Process, you establish a pattern of continual growth. By living in this manner, you are always expanding your experience base, building on your strengths, and fortifying your self-confidence. That is why it is so important to learn to view failure as merely a lesson learned, a helpful marker that gives you a grasp for what you can and cannot do *at that point* in your life.

I was writing little plays back in seventh grade; I imagined myself a great writer. I showed a couple of the plays to my teacher and she didn't know what to say. I think she was embarrassed by them; she obviously saw nothing of merit in them. Looking back at those early ventures, I don't see much merit in them, either—except that I was learning my voice, honing my craft. I was learning the trade, so to speak.

Pretty much everything I wrote in high school and college was, in a literary sense, trash. But I was learning, probing, trying new techniques and ways, taking greater risks, and forever building upon what I can happily call my "failures." From my "failures" came my plays that even my seventh-grade teacher could be proud of.

Amanda, age 27, accomplished playwright

■ Your Risk-Taking Profile

How are you at taking risks? Answer the following questions to determine your willingness to take risks.

1. What is the one risk you could take today that would move you most efficiently and effectively toward fulfilling your vision of a better life?

_____

_____

2. What is the one thing you fear the most about taking that risk?

_____

_____

3. What one habit or thing holds you back from taking that risk?

_____

_____

4. How would taking this risk change your life?

_____

_____

Identify two risks you have taken during the last year.
Risk 1:

_____

Risk 2:

_____

Now select one of those risks and answer the following questions related to your decision to take that risk.

1. Your goal in taking this risk was:

_____

_____

2. Your backup plan if things did not work out was:

_____

_____

_____

3. The people who supported you in taking this risk were:

_____

_____

_____

4. Taking that risk resulted in:

_____

_____

_____

Complete the following sentences regarding this risk.
I had the courage to face my fears in taking this risk because . . .

_____

_____

I believed in my ability to overcome obstacles and solve problems in taking this risk because . . .

_____

_____

I was willing to experience failure in this risk because . . .

_____

_____

Now answer the questions about taking risks in general.
In matters that are important to me, I face my fears and take risks . . .

Always   Usually   Sometimes   Once in a while   Never

I believe in my ability to overcome obstacles and solve problems in taking risks . . .

Always   Usually   Sometimes   Once in a while   Never

I am willing to experience failure in taking risks . . .

Always   Usually   Sometimes   Once in a while   Never

Looking before You Leap

Taking risks is essential to living a fulfilling and successful life, but I'm not saying that you blindly enter into a risk on a whim. You need to consider the risk and its consequences, and to take on that risk with confidence. Taking risks takes courage, belief in yourself, and a willingness to fail. It also takes wisdom and faith.

Taking a risk is like leaping over an obstacle or a chasm that separates you from what you want. If you are certain that the risk is worth it, you can make that leap with determination, enthusiasm, and focus. But if you aren't so sure, you won't be as determined, enthusiastic, and focused, and in all likelihood, you won't make it. Instead of taking opportunities as they appear, you will be torn by inde-

cision and ambivalence. Should you run for student council or not? Should you go out for track or not? Should you try out for this play or not? Indecision can be a dangerous attitude. In every wildlife documentary I've ever seen, the predator always gets the one animal that can't decide which way to run.

Now, you aren't impalas running from the lions, so you can take time to evaluate the risks you take. Make sure the risk is in line with your principles, values, and beliefs before you make the leap. Measure the costs versus the gains. The more valued the gain, the more willing you should be to risk the cost. You might not be elected for student council. But if serving on student council is meaningful to you, and you believe that you will gain from the experience, then you'll risk the time and effort you'll need to put into a campaign, as well as the feelings you'll have to deal with if you aren't elected. You might do poorly in track, you'll have to be committed to attending practice daily, and the training will not be easy. But if you have a great desire to excel in this sport, then you'll lay it on the line. You might not be cast for the play you audition for. But if theater and acting are important to you, and you want to "step into your outer limits here," you'll weigh the potential good versus the reality that you might not be chosen—this time.

No matter the situation, you need to consider the potential good that can come out of taking the risk, how it might positively affect goals you have and the vision you have for your life, and weigh that against the costs involved. Some risks, as you evaluate them, may not be worth your time, but others—even if you see a slim chance for immediate payback—may be worth taking, because you'll learn from the process, even if it turns out to be a "failure." Remember Edison and the lightbulb.

Overcoming Fear

You might say, "I've calculated the risk involved and I really want to take it because I really think it's worth it, but I'm still stuck." I'd respond that most likely you're stuck in fear.

You cannot live your life out of fear of what might happen. You must live out of your vision for a better life. The greatest reason people do not take risks is fear of the unknown. The greatest way to overcome fear is to face it.

To face fear, you need faith and courage. You have to have faith that there really is no bogeyman under the bed, and the courage to look down there to confirm it. Fears can haunt and control you when you lack faith in your ability to overcome them and the courage to take them on. Fear defeats you when you allow it to condition your mind, to make you a coward.

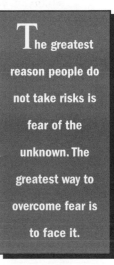

The greatest reason people do not take risks is fear of the unknown. The greatest way to overcome fear is to face it.

Have you ever been forced by an emergency to do something you were afraid to do, something you never thought you could do? Have you ever leaped higher or run faster than you ever thought you could because *you knew you had to do it?* That is the form of energy you need to tap into to overcome your fear of taking risks. You have to develop a sort of *crisis mentality* to summon the courage to overcome such fears. You have to decide that taking this risk is vital to your life. Remember that fear grows when you hide from it, but it usually shrinks when you face it and learn about it and challenge it head on.

My first semester of college was a little like jumping into a pool of ice-cold water. You may know it's cold, but nothing can really prepare you for the initial shock. I was only 16 and it was a lot of firsts for me: first time picking my own classes and schedule, first time riding a bus, and first time not knowing anyone in my classes.

It was a definite stretch of my comfort zone. I am, unfortunately, prone to nervousness. My heartbeat quickens and my stomach aches, and it's frustrating because it's hard to control. What helped me the most was my daily devotions. Communing with God in the morning before class calmed my spirit and put things into proper perspective (it's not a life-threatening thing to be a few minutes late to class). With that nervousness gone, I can function properly, getting everything out of my classes that I can.

Kelli, age 16

131

We all have fears. Studies have identified more than a hundred fears, ranging from fear of open spaces to fear of closed spaces, from fear of heights to fear of depths. We're afraid of spiders, snakes, and mosquitoes. Remember this, though: Fear is a learned response. We are not born with it; that is why parents have to watch their young children so closely. Fears that are learned can be un-learned. A child who fears dogs because a mean dog chased her can learn to like dogs if exposed to friendly ones. Fears are real only when we make them real by investing too much into them. When we allow fear to dominate our lives, we give it too much power. Often, fear is the only thing that stands between us and our vision for a successful life, and if we don't develop the courage to over-come those fears, we might never have the opportunity to reach our dreams and goals.

■ Calculating Risk and Overcoming Fear

Your ability to take risks depends on your decision-making skills and on your ap-proach to risk taking. First, you have to understand what needs, desires, and val-ues motivate your behavior. If you aren't certain of your goals and clear in your vision for your life, then you are ill-prepared to take risks that will move you toward those goals.

Before taking risks, then, check your vision and evaluate whether the risk you are considering is in line with your values. Are you considering taking the risk for good reason or for ego? Is the risk appealing to you because it will help you lead a better, more worthwhile and challenging life, or will it simply mean more money, more prestige, or more physical gratification?

Think about a risk you are considering taking and answer these ques-tions about it:

1. What lies on the other side? If you take this risk, how will it affect your goals and your vision for yourself?

_____

_____

_____

2. Will it strengthen the important areas of your life—your relationships, your ed-ucational pursuits, your personal development, and so on—or will it weaken any of these aspects?

_____

_____

_____

3. Why does the risk appeal to you?

_____

_____

_____

4. Write down what you stand to gain.

_____

_____

5. Write down what you stand to lose.

_____

_____

6. Now weigh the potential gain against the downside and ask yourself, *Will this move me closer to fulfilling my vision for my life, or could it potentially set me back?*

_____

_____

One method for gaining the faith and confidence necessary to take on your fears is to purposely confront your fears. Here are a few questions to help you face and overcome a fear.

Name a fear that you have—one that keeps you from taking risks that you feel you should probably take to be successful.

Why is this a fear for you?

_____

_____

How can you overcome it? Consider practical steps to take, resources, and people who can offer assistance.

_____

_____

List one action you intend to take this week to reduce the impact of this fear.

_____

_____

133

The Slide for Life

There was a boy who grew up in the South Bronx to immigrant Jamaican parents. He was not a particularly good student; he was an average athlete, and not overly ambitious as a young man. He seemed to find himself, though, when he joined the ROTC in high school. He discovered leadership abilities that he didn't know he had possessed. So he set his sights on a military career.

But then early in his basic training, he met a challenge that forced him to overcome a fear or give up on his dream. It was called, dramatically enough, "The Slide for Life." It was a cable strung a hundred feet above a river between two trees. It started high in one tree and dropped steeply to the tree on the other side of the river. The young soldier had to ride down that cable on a hook attached to a pulley that ran along it. He was not allowed to let go, falling safely into the river, until the instructor issued the command at the very last second before he would crash into the tree.

It was "the moment I had my first doubt about the career I had chosen," Colin Powell later wrote in his autobiography, *My American Journey.* "It was one of the most frightening experiences of my life."

But he did it. He overcame his doubts and fears and took the risk because he knew it was a necessary step in his pursuit of a career in the military. Had he chickened out or refused to face his fears, it is doubtful that Colin Powell would have succeeded in the military. His same willingness to take risks later resulted in Powell's applying for a White House fellowship that propelled him to even higher levels as the national security adviser to the president of the United States and, eventually, chairman of the Joint Chiefs of Staff.

Colin Powell realizes that there is no progress without struggle. You will never get to the next level if you don't widen your experience and base of knowledge, and often that involves taking risks.

As Powell was preparing to take his "Slide for Life," he had to overcome a lot of fear. Regardless of the area of life or particular pursuit, remember these key points for overcoming fear and taking risks:

- The most important risks to take are those that will move you most quickly toward your goals.
- Failure to take risks limits your opportunities and new experiences.
- By avoiding risks, you are giving in to fears and missing opportunities.
- Failure can provide an opportunity to learn. Some of the most useful lessons are learned as a result of things that didn't work out.
- In order to evaluate a risk, balance your needs and desires with your goals and values.

- You can manage fear when you have faith in your ability to solve problems.
- If you focus on your fears rather than on your goals, you miss opportunities and fail to achieve your vision.

Learning from Failure and Criticism

I just mentioned that failure can provide opportunities to learn. Earlier, when I described the attributes you need to be a risk taker, I talked about Thomas Edison's many failures that he turned into success. You also heard about a playwright who learned from her early failures. Understand this about success: For every successful person you can find, you can also find a number of failures from which that person learned along the way.

Identify someone you consider to be successful and ask that person how many failures he or she had before success came. I guarantee you that any successful person had to learn failure before success. That is what learning is all about: doing it wrong to get it right. We don't all succeed at everything we try. Most of us go through failure to reach success, just as we go through fear in order to build courage. Ralph Waldo Emerson said, "Do the thing you fear, and the death of fear is certain."

Weight lifting is the simplest example I can think of to illustrate the process of going through failure to reach success. In fact, fitness instructors often talk about "going for failure." Now that sounds like fun, doesn't it? *Let's go fail!* What does that mean? In weightlifting, to go for failure means to push yourself to the limit, to lift as much as you can as many times as you can until you can't lift anymore. Why do you do that? To build muscle, you first break it down, exhaust it, and then build new strength into it. By going for failure, you are preparing your muscles for greater success.

In weight lifting, as in life, failure is nothing more than a part of growing and building strength. Don't think of a failure as permanent. If you do that, you give failure too much power over your life. But if you put failure in its proper place as simply a step in the Success Process, you empower yourself to take life on.

Look at one of the most successful athletes in history, Michael Jordan. He wasn't afraid of failure when he left basketball at the peak of his career and tried his skills at baseball. It was something he wanted to do with his life. He wanted to try and he wanted to succeed. But he didn't fear failure as some permanent condition. In fact, he did fail to make it as a professional baseball player, but I haven't heard anyone describe Michael as a loser or a failure. He experienced failure, as we all do at one time or another, but he moved on with his dynamic life, looking for new challenges. This is why, in the second half of Jordan's basketball career, his opponents frequently talked more about his *mental* toughness than his *physical* skills. Michael, they said, can beat you through his sheer force of will. Wouldn't it be great to have people say the same thing about you?

Now, if Jordan had viewed his life only in terms of whether or not he made it as a professional baseball player, he would have been a failure. But as a wise, optimistic, and self-motivated person, Jordan understood that life is a process, and that failure can be a part of it. One thing Jordan did not fear, obviously, was criticism from others. But many people *are* paralyzed by a fear of being criticized. *What will people say? What will they think about me? How can I handle their criticism?* If you listen to that voice, you will do nothing.

> When I was a little kid, I begged and begged my parents to let me take saxophone lessons. I thought music—especially jazz—was the coolest thing. They finally let me take lessons when I was in sixth grade. And you know what? I was pretty bad. But I still loved it. I thought, I'll become a great musician some day, do my own recordings. Get a big contract, the whole gig.
>
> But the thing is, I lived in a tough neighborhood. Let's just put it this way: the friends I grew up with weren't into music, at least not to play. To listen to, yeah, but to spend time *playing* music was . . . it was a "sissy" thing, something a guy like me wasn't supposed to do. It was like this macho thing. Guys just didn't do it.
>
> So after about a year I stopped. The funny thing was, my friends really never said too much to me about playing. They made fun of me a little, but it was mainly what I *thought* they were thinking about me. It was like, I had to make a choice: them or the saxophone.
>
> Kendall, age 16

If you wait around for everyone you know to approve everything you do, you'll still be waiting when the lights go out for the last time. This is called *paralysis by analysis.* If those closest to you are critical of a risk you plan to take, listen to them, weigh their advice for what it is worth, and then do what you think is best based on your evaluation of all aspects of your life. Just as it is important to view failure as a step in the process of success, it is important also to handle criticism in a constructive manner.

Let's say one of your teachers names you a group leader for a class project that spans a couple of months. But halfway into the project, your teacher pulls you aside one Friday and says she may have to replace you as group leader because your group hasn't progressed; your project is way behind. She says you're coasting, goofing around, while the other groups are making good progress.

Ouch. That sort of criticism can make for a long weekend. Or maybe not. Maybe, just maybe, it could *energize* you to push yourself to the outer limits of your abilities, making your teacher happy, and perhaps you could learn a lesson that can expand your potential for bettering your life.

Here are three very different responses that you could have to the criticism delivered by your teacher. Which one of them is the healthiest and most beneficial?

1. *I'm worthless and I'm weak.*

   Your teacher's words weigh on you like a waterbed mattress dumped on your back. They get heavier and heavier as the negative thoughts flow in. *I'm in over my head. I can't lead this project. I'm a screwup.* Overwhelmed by negative thoughts, you sink into depression and spend the weekend lying on the couch and feeling sorry for yourself. When you do drag yourself back to school, your teacher sees immediately that you have not taken her words to heart and she replaces you as group leader. This response is self-defeating and rooted in a negative approach to life. Criticism is viewed as the end result, the killing blow.

2. *This teacher has never liked me. I don't like how she treats me.*

   As soon as the teacher walks away, you throw your backpack across the room and stomp out. When you get home, you kick the cat over the neighbor's fence, hand out insults to family members like candy at Halloween, and make everyone's life miserable. Anger—seething, boiling, red-faced anger—has you in its hold. You spend the weekend building yourself into a full rage, charge into school on Monday morning like an ugly storm, and yell at the teacher for "doing you wrong." She responds by pointing the way to the principal's office. You have taken her criticism as a personal affront, and it has poisoned your judgment.

3. *What can I do to get back on track?*

   Instead of taking the criticism as a knife to the heart or as a personal insult, you take it as an opportunity to review and improve your performance as a group leader. *Is there truth in what my teacher said? How have I done compared to the other group leaders? What are they doing that I am not doing? What can I do to show my teacher that I am committed to improving?* You go home in a contemplative mood, sobered by the criticism, but not defeated by it. You spend the weekend doing constructive things while also weighing the best approach to the week ahead. You go back to school on Monday and tell your teacher that you have taken her criticism to heart, and that you are going to rededicate yourself to your duties as group leader. You have used criticism as a building block.

Many teenagers fear criticism because they place so much emphasis on being accepted. We all want to be liked. We all want to please other people. The problem is maintaining a balance between controlling our own lives and winning the acceptance and approval of the people we care about. Most teenagers want to fit in and be accepted by their peers, and as a result, they find themselves at that fork in the road, choosing whether to do what they think is right or to do what will win others' approval.

I wish they taught classes in this in junior high to prepare people. It takes courage to face criticism or rejection from your peers, and it is so easy to ignore your own conscience and good judgment when others are pressuring you to go along to get along. Peer pressure and the desire to be accepted can often end with traumatic results. In Florida not long ago, a group of teenagers went on a criminal rampage that began with vandalism but ended with them murdering a high school band instructor. The teens were mostly good students who had given up their own good judgment to follow a classmate who had become their leader.

It's a frightening thing, and not uncommon, for one person with bad intentions to corrupt others into following him. Often, it begins when someone is afraid to face criticism from a friend or acquaintance. You have to have faith in your own judgment and in your own value as a person in these—and in all—circumstances.

I have a friend who was rejected by the in crowd in high school because he refused to go along with things that they were doing. He took a lot of heat over it, but a few years later a girl he had gone to school with told him how much she had come to admire him for standing up for what he thought was right. Needless to say, my friend has done well in this world because of his faith in his own judgment and his ability to take a stand when necessary. On the other hand, those young people in Florida have done things that they and their loved ones will have to pay for probably for the rest of their lives.

It is also true in relationships that some people are so eager to please and to be loved that they give away too much of themselves. They let the other person dominate them, even hurt them physically because they are so eager to have a relationship and to feel loved. It is often difficult to find the middle road in these situations, particularly for someone who has not been grounded in a loving and secure family life at home. But it is vital to pro-

> Many teenagers fear criticism because they place so much emphasis on being accepted. We all want to be liked. We all want to please other people. The problem is maintaining a balance between controlling our own lives and winning the acceptance and approval of the people we care about.

tect yourself in these situations so that you are not taken advantage of. You have value. You deserve to be respected. No one has the right to abuse you mentally or physically. Chances are better that no one will if you take steps to take control of your life. We'll talk about doing that after the next worksheet.

■ Turning Negatives into Positives

Think back to when you learned how to ride a bike. How many times did you go out and try to ride that bike and fail? How many times did you skin your knees or bite the dirt? But each of those failures contributed to your eventual success, didn't they? (Don't tell me you still are riding around with the training wheels on!)

Write down a recent success that came out of failure.

My success was _____

Now write down the failure(s) that preceded that success. _____

_____

_____ .

Now think about the way you have handled criticism in the past. Recall the example in the text about the group leader who was on the hot seat. That group leader had choices: to be depressed and sulk, to be angry and lash out, or to take the criticism to heart and decide to improve. How do you respond when you're criticized?

First consider a time when you did not respond so well to constructive criticism and complete the following sentences.

I was criticized for _____ .

My response to the criticism was _____

_____ .

The result of my response was _____

_____ .

Now recall a time when you responded in a more healthy and productive manner to constructive criticism and complete the following sentences.

I was criticized for _____ .

My response to the criticism was _____

_____ .

The result of my response was _____

_____.

Now answer this final question: How might the result of the first criticism been different had you responded in a better way? _____

_____.

Taking Control of Your Life

Don't allow your peers to dictate to you how to live your life, particularly if they have not established that they have your best interests at heart. Believe me, it is worth the risk to face criticism and rejection if it means keeping your self-respect. Are you giving up too much to please others and to avoid criticism? I'd say you are *if:*

> **I**t is worth the risk to face criticism and rejection if it means keeping your self-respect.

- You are trying to get people to like you rather than to respect you.
- You do things you know are wrong simply to gain approval.
- You do something you really don't want to do for someone who doesn't really have your best interests at heart.
- It seems like you can't do enough to please someone.
- A friendship or relationship seems more like work than fun.

Here are five things to strive for in handling criticism, risking disapproval, and taking control of your life.

1. *Take pleasure in being in control of your own life.*

Unless you enjoy wearing a sign on your back that says Kick me, you should take pleasure in running your own life. Don't cater to the whims of others. Be thoughtful of other people and their needs, but only because you want to, not because they demand it. You give up too much of yourself when you forfeit control of your life to others by catering to their demands or trying to live up to their expectations rather than your own.

2. *Feel free to express your uniqueness and your own needs.*

There is so much pressure to fit in with the crowd. I encourage you to express your own talents and gifts and to celebrate them without feeling pressure to wear the same clothes, do the same things, and to follow the crowd even if you don't care to. If blending in makes you feel more comfortable, fine, but don't submerge your own personality to win approval.

3. *Don't feel guilty about saying No.*

This one isn't in the Ten Commandments or the U.S. Constitution, but it bears the same weight. You have the right to say no and the responsibility to say no if that is what you judge to be the proper response. You may not be correct. You may be the only one. It may make you unpopular. But it is your right. Have no fear; have no guilt; say no whenever and wherever you judge it to be in your best interest. People can argue with your judgment, but it is your right to make that judgment.

4. *Let them know where you stand, loudly and proudly.*

Don't be afraid to take a stand or to let people know that you have taken a stand. No one respects a wishy-washy person. Don't force your opinions on other people. Don't expect others to applaud every time you offer an opinion. But feel free to exercise your free will, and to let others know that you are willing to take a stand even when it might not be popular.

5. *Be curious about life and all that it has to offer you.*

Too often, we pull back from things that interest us for fear that we will be criticized by other people. *Classical music? That's for nerds. You're working with the handicapped? What are you, a do-gooder?* Some of the things I enjoy the most now are things that initially I was afraid to risk trying simply because I didn't want to appear inept or to face criticism. Feel free to check out the things that interest *you.* If someone else doesn't like it, that's too bad.

■ Standing Up for Who You Are

The ability to take control of your life can help you step into your own outer limits. How good are you at taking control? Circle "True" or "False" for each of the following statements.

1. I rarely cater to the whims of others. If someone asks me to do something, I usually base my decision on whether it's right for me.
True   False

2. I am much more concerned about living up to my own expectations than the expectations of others.
True   False

3. I'm not concerned with fitting in with the in crowd.
True   False

4. I feel proud of my uniqueness and who I am as a person.
True   False

5. I don't give in to peer pressure. I can say no when I need to.

                            True   False

6. When I say no to something my friends want me to do, and I know it was the right decision, I don't feel guilty about it.

                            True   False

7. I can take a stand on something that I feel strongly about.

                            True   False

8. I'd rather be ridiculed or rejected than do something stupid, illegal, or immoral.

                            True   False

9. I pursue my interests even if they aren't judged "cool" by others.

                            True   False

10. I try new things even if I think I might be inept at first.

                            True   False

Now rate yourself:

1–3 "True" answers: You're letting others control your life.

4–6 "True" answers: You're gaining control of your life in some areas, but need to work on it in other areas.

7–8 "True" answers: You're in good control of your life.

9–10 "True" answers: You're in great control of your life and are wise and mature beyond your years!

Now that you've learned how to step into the outer limits, take well-calculated risks, and learn from failure and criticism, you're ready to take the next step: adapting to change. Most people dislike change. But you can make it work *for* you, rather than *against* you, in the Success Process. Read on.

7 Pilot the Seasons of Change

The most effective way to cope with change is to help create it.

L. W. Lynett

The Midwest, and Chicago in particular, are known to experience frequent and abrupt weather changes. "Don't like the weather? Just hang on for five minutes. It'll change." Or so the saying goes.

Change happens. It happens to everyone throughout his or her life. It happens whether you seek it or not; it happens whether you are following your vision or not; it happens whether you are stepping into your outer limits or not. What's important is how you respond to change. Don't fool yourself into thinking you can avoid it, because you can't.

You may want to feel in control of your life, but the reality is you can't control everything. Some people have a great fear of change. Many times this is due to the fear of the unknown, stepping outside a comfort zone, being forced to try new things that you'd really rather not try. Have you ever been there? Phanedra Harper has. Let me tell you a piece of her story.

Phanedra was fourteen years old when a change her mother forced her to undergo made her extremely nervous. The Chicago teenager, who lives in a public housing project, was not doing well in her crowded public school. She was a fairly capable student, but her teachers were forced to deal with many distractions, including the threat of gang violence. Students like Phanedra often get lost in the shuffle in such situations, like a person with a minor wound entering an emergency room full of people who have been critically wounded.

But Phanedra's mother dreamed that her daughter would make it to college and find a better life, so she brought about a change. She enrolled Phanedra in an after-school program at the Metro Achievement Center, a federally sponsored educational facility designed to help inner-city girls get into Chicago's best high schools.

Phanedra was so nervous about making the change that when she first entered the Metro program, she was afraid to speak. But within a few months, she was not only speaking freely, she was pulling As and Bs instead of Bs and Cs. Phanedra's response to change resulted in her getting into one of Chicago's best high schools.

Let me tell you one more story about change. Put yourself in the shoes of Matt and consider how you would respond to the change he went through. Matt was a two-year starter on his high school basketball team heading into his senior year. He was a good player with a good work ethic and attitude. The team always seemed to have a lot of potential, but they never went anywhere with it. A new coach was brought in shortly before Matt's senior year. This coach had seen the team play a number of times over the past few years, and he was highly critical of its attitudes, its lack of teamwork, and its whole approach to the game. He believed in a very different system and a different approach to coaching than what the team was used to.

So this coach shook things up. He kicked a couple of seniors off the squad before the first game had been played, after warning them about their bad attitudes. He benched every starter, including Matt, and said he was going with the younger guys, because that was their future. He was doing this in part to challenge the seniors, but most of them did not respond well to that challenge.

Anger and resentment were the most common responses. There were many heated discussions in the locker room. Several players threatened to quit and the coach encouraged them to do so if they weren't going to play his way.

Although it is normal to experience emotional reactions to change, people often get so caught up in those emotions that they lose their way temporarily and make poor decisions that can have a lasting impact.

Want to know how Matt responded? Read on. And as you do, you'll learn how to

- understand the natural process of change,
- navigate the seasons, or stages, of change,
- seek change, rather than just letting it happen, and
- manage change, including controlling your anger, developing patience, and handling stress.

The message in this chapter is simple: To be successful, you have to learn how to adapt to change, how to not be defeated by it or fear it, how to make it work for you. To make it work for you, you first have to understand the process.

Understanding the Process of Change

Change is a part of life. Seasons change; people grow; fads come and go; dynasties crumble; beauty withers; caterpillars become butterflies; landscapes change; and on and on. You are not the same person you were a year ago. You have experienced more and, hopefully, have learned and grown wiser. You are honing your talents as a pianist or a point guard or a poet. You have most likely made changes, subtly or not so subtly, in your physical appearance, your emotional makeup, your spiritual grounding, your intellectual base. Change is all around you, and you are part of that change.

Not all change is unwelcome or hard to handle. For instance, maybe your hard work over the past year to improve your skills as a point guard has been rewarded with a starting position. That's a change that you most likely will gladly accept, even if you have some concern about starting.

Other change, however, is harder: the loss of a loved one, a breakup of a relationship, the loss of your ability to do something you love. For instance, let's say you're that point guard who has finally earned the right to start. On the eve of the first game, you severely sprain your ankle and will be out for several games. *That* change is much harder to deal with, but no less a part of life than the more desired changes.

Sometimes people react to change in their lives as though it is a rare and shocking experience. But our entire lives are a cycle of constant change, seasons of change, as reflected in this beautiful and familiar passage from Ecclesiastes:

145

To every thing there is a season, and a time to every purpose under the heaven:

A time to be born, and a time to die; a time to plant, and a time to pluck up that which is planted;

A time to kill, and a time to heal; a time to break down, and a time to build up;

A time to weep, and a time to laugh; a time to mourn, and a time to dance;

A time to cast away stones, and a time to gather stones together; a time to embrace and a time to refrain from embracing;

A time to get, and a time to lose; a time to keep, and a time to cast away;

A time to rend, and a time to sew; a time to keep silence, and a time to speak;

A time to love, and a time to hate; a time of war, and a time of peace.

Navigating the Seasons of Change

Change, then, is not an *event*. It is a *natural process*, like the change of seasons in nature. The four seasons can be likened to four stages of change, during which your emotional responses may range from a sense of loss and sadness, to a feeling of disorientation and lethargy, to gradual rejuvenation and exhilaration. These emotions mirror, in many ways, the moods and emotions that accompany the changing seasons in nature. The four stages of change are:

1. Letting go of old things to welcome in new things,
2. Sticking to plans to change even when you feel anxious,
3. Holding tight during the ups and-downs of change, and
4. Blossoming and growing through change.

The reality is that we are at different stages of change in different areas of our lives all the time. For instance, you may be struggling to let go of an old relationship, but you may be blossoming academically like you never realized you could, brought about by an excellent teacher who makes learning fun. In yet another area, you might be just holding on as a new student has, at least temporarily, supplanted you in your role on the wrestling team.

However, change *can* often occur in the chronological order just described: letting go of old things, sticking to plans to change, holding on tight, and finally blossoming. To use an extreme example, consider a young girl who has never ridden on a merry-go-round alone before; her mother has always accompanied her, using her hand to lightly balance her daughter as she rode. This time, however, the young girl is determined to ride alone. She holds her mother's hand all the way to the merry-go-round before finally, reluctantly, *letting go.* She looks at the horse in front of her, then back at her mother; she obviously is feeling anxious about her decision and wants to turn back. But she resolutely *sticks to her plan,* gets on the horse, and *holds on* as the ride goes around and around. The first few times around, she just holds on, not even smiling at her mother. But after a little bit she relaxes and begins to smile. By the time she gets off the merry-go-round, she is beaming. She has just made a significant change in her life, and she *has grown* through the experience.

> The reality is that we are at different stages of change in different areas of our lives all the time.

No doubt you've struggled—and grown—through many changes in your life. Let's take a look at each stage of change to see how you can better adapt and use the change for your own good.

Stage One: Letting Go

Have you ever been excited about a certain change coming, yet felt sad over what was ending? That's how many people describe their high school graduation (though it's also true that there are those who are not sad at all to leave high school!). These mixed emotions you may have experienced in "letting go" are quite common. The end of summer and the beginning of another school year often bring with it these mixed emotions as does the end of a difficult class in which you made some unexpected gains. On the one hand, you breathe a sigh of relief that the class is over; with your next breath you feel a strange sadness that you will be leaving the class that brought so much challenge—and growth.

Many times, this is the stage of change that people have the hardest time handling. As many of Matt's teammates showed, it is not easy

to let go of the comfortable and familiar. How many times have you held on to some habit or some way of life that you knew wasn't that good for you, and a better way was awaiting you? You want to change, yet you don't want to let go.

Just as trees cut off nourishment to their leaves in the fall, the process of change begins with the act of letting go of that part of life we want to change. If the trees didn't release their old leaves, their branches would not be able to sprout buds for new growth. The same is true for you and me. Our personal growth can only come when we let go of old ways and self-defeating behavior that has held us back.

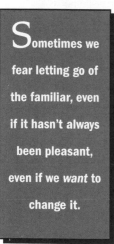

> It's weird, but I was afraid to change my attitude for the better. I'd sort of had this reputation as having this bad attitude, and I finally realized I was getting nowhere with it—the person I was really hurting with it was myself. So I really *wanted* to change, but it was like, if I change my attitude, I've lost this part of me, this part that sort of defined who I was. And that was scary. Even though I knew the change would be for the better, I felt like I was losing something that, in a way, was really valuable.
>
> Anita, age 15

In any change, something is lost, whether planned or unplanned, whether good or bad. That is a fact that many people have difficulty dealing with when faced with change. As much as they may want to change their lives, they don't want to let go of what they have. It's like the young girl facing the merry-go-round, wanting to ride alone, but afraid to. There are times when we have to let go of what is comfortable and supporting—in the girl's case, her mother's hand—and take on the challenge of change.

> Sometimes we fear letting go of the familiar, even if it hasn't always been pleasant, even if we *want* to change it.

Sometimes we fear letting go of the familiar, even if it hasn't always been pleasant, even if we *want* to change it. Don't let those feelings stop you from going through with changes that can open the possibilities to a better life. When I left Bob Brown's public relations firm to strike out on my own, I was full of fear. I really knew nothing about running my own business. I had enjoyed working with him. But I wanted to make a leap in my pursuit of a dream to have my own business in Chicago, so I accepted my fears and concerns as a natural part of the process of change, and then went ahead. In your own pursuits, remember this: You may not know how to get where you want to go, but don't let that stop you. You won't find your way out of a maze by standing still or looking back. If you move about it is more likely that the way will reveal itself.

When Matt's teammates reacted to changes on the team with fear and anger, they weren't wrong in responding with their emotions, but they were too focused on what they were leaving. They would have been better off focusing on what was ahead of them. The truth was, as soon as the new coach came in, their old way of doing things was over. The approach to practices and games was totally different, and the players would not survive with their old approach. They should have recognized that change was inevitable and made the best of it. To respond any other way was self-defeating.

Here are a few suggestions on what you can do to help yourself let go of the past in order to make positive changes in your life.

- *Tune in to your emotions.* Monitor your feelings and your attitudes toward those around you. Don't allow your emotions to cloud your judgment or to spark negative behavior.
- *Recognize that sadness and anger are common feelings brought about initially by change.* There is no need to fight these feelings. That only brings more turmoil. Take the sadness or anger and channel it into positive energy by accepting it and understanding why you feel the way you do. If you are sad, do something that makes you laugh or elevates your mood. If you are angry, use that energy to do something constructive that you've been putting off, such as exercising or working on a class project.
- *Acknowledge your feelings and any sense of loss.* Put your moods into perspective and grant yourself permission to feel sad or angry or whatever you feel. There is no reason to feel guilty or angry at yourself for having perfectly valid emotions.
- *Say good-bye.* Do this in your own way to the people, places, and things that will be left behind. Accept what has happened, acknowledge how you feel about it, and embrace the change that has resulted.

Stage Two: Sticking to Your Plans

Oftentimes shortly after you let go of something while making a change, you feel sad, stagnant, or lost. You may feel as though you have made a mistake in giving up the old and chancing something new. This is a natural reaction at this stage of the change process. Rosabeth Moss Kanter, author of *The Change Masters,* was referring to this when she wrote that "every change looks like failure in the middle."

It is natural to feel anxious when making a change. Think again of that little girl and how anxious she felt before she decided to get on that merry-go-round by herself. When you find yourself anxious, understand and acknowledge your anxiety but don't despair. Stick with your plans to pursue a better life. You may want to give up or go back to the old way, but you have to be courageous when you are chasing a dream.

> **G**et together with people who stoke your confidence and inspire you to improve yourself.

Give yourself credit for having put enough thought into your decision to change *before* you took the action. This is no time for second thoughts or looking over your shoulder. This is the period for moving resolutely ahead, for having faith in yourself and your decision to change. Not to frighten you, but it could be disastrous to turn back on your decision at this point because you have already altered your old situation by leaving it. The way things were no longer exist. It is better to follow through and to look ahead.

Use this time to sort out feelings and reflect on your needs, values, and desires while gathering strength and resolve for the new beginning about to come. Here are a few suggestions to help you more effectively manage this period in the change process:

- *Take time to recharge your energy levels.* Build up strength to face the changes that will bring you closer to the life you want for yourself. Read motivational and inspirational books and biographies and writings of successful people, particularly those who have had experiences that you can relate to. Listen to inspirational and motivational tapes. Get together with people who stoke your confidence and inspire you to improve yourself. Get together with dynamic people who are taking life on.

- *Keep a journal.* Record in it your thoughts on where you have been in your life and where you want to go. Keeping a journal helps you express thoughts and feelings that you might not be conscious of otherwise. You don't have to record every thought. Just a page a day is a good start, although as you progress, you may find yourself writing more and more. A journal can help you sort out the feelings and find the resolve to stick with your plan.

- *Talk with friends, family, and any mentors or role models you have.* Discuss with them the changes that you need to make. You don't have to ask their advice; they may not even agree with what you are doing. But it is helpful to talk to come to a more complete understanding of your own feelings toward what is going on in your life and why a change is important to stick with.

Stage Three: Holding on Tight

While Matt spent little time fretting over the changes going on with his basketball team, many of his teammates were angry and upset. But after a few months, they began to feel more comfortable in the coach's new system and

in their new roles within that system. Many of them came around to actually liking the new system better, and wishing they had been in that system all along. That often happens when you persevere and work your way through change. If you hang in there, often you come to a point when you adjust and then take pride in successfully managing the change.

Remember the young girl on the merry-go-round? Once the merry-go-round began spinning, she held on tight; she was probably equal parts excitement and fright as she experienced the ride for the first time alone. There is, in this stage, a roller-coaster effect on the emotions. Part of you loves the exhilaration and adrenaline rush of change; the other part is screaming, "What am I doing? Am I *nuts?*"

Our art teacher sort of commissioned several of us to do this huge mural on one of the walls of our school gym. He said it had to depict school spirit and combine the idea of sports with education. That is, that sports and education are tied together, and that they shouldn't be seen as separate, especially in school. And of course it had to be very creative and cool.

So he was asking for volunteers to work on the mural. I thought that was cool so I volunteered. But then he asked for someone to take charge of the whole thing, to be the "project director," so to speak. No one raised their hand. I don't know why, but I finally did. Not 'cause I felt forced, but because I really wanted to.

A little later it sunk in: what have I done to myself? Why did I get myself into this? To *help* with the mural would be easy enough—and fun. To *direct* the whole project . . . yikes!

Jackie, age 18

Change can be scary. It's like taking an advanced algebra class. At first you wish you had opted for the regular class, and you may struggle with the first few quizzes; but eventually the learning clicks in, you adjust to the work, and a new level of comfort begins to be established.

As I moved from a sports marketing business to a more diverse business, I often wondered if it was the right thing to do. It was scary and at times I was a little down about whether it was going to work; but, suddenly, things began to fall together rapidly. I've since established a business presence in New York as well as Chicago, and the opportunities are coming from all directions. This change in my approach to business has taken on a life of its own. It is exhilarating and challenging just to keep up with it all.

This is when your vision is put to the test. This is when you find out whether you are really on track to your dream. Everything seems accelerated, every emotion accentuated. You feel more alive than ever before. It is a time that requires thoughtful handling. Otherwise, you can get swept away by all of the rapid developments and lose focus or feel overwhelmed.

Here are some things you can do to help manage this phase of change:

- *Stop planning and get into action.* Things begin to happen now because you have laid the groundwork and made your decision. Now is the time to take advantage of the opportunities that open up. It can be daunting when change begins to ignite all around you, but this is when you want to act upon your dreams.
- *Be prepared to expand your vision.* Keep in mind that you may need to adjust your vision for a better life to fit the growth you are undergoing. You may need to set your sights even higher than before to allow for that growth. You certainly don't want to stop one day and look back and say, "I

missed that opportunity to move to an even higher level." At the very least, you want to be alert to the fact that as your opportunities grow, you need to grow, too.

- *Take it step by step.* In this period of rapid change, that may mean you'll be stepping along at a brisk pace, if not sprinting! But keep in mind earlier lessons on setting direction for your vision so that you always stay on course.
- *Stay focused on your primary goals.* There will be many temptations and distractions at this point of the change process, so you need to remind yourself of your ultimate goal. That doesn't mean that you can't explore other opportunities, but always ask yourself: *Is that where I want to go with my life?*
- *Take care of your life.* In such an exhilarating time, it is easy to focus on the change process and neglect other aspects of your life. Remember that a balanced life includes maintaining healthy situations in your relationships, your personal development, and your school life.

Stage Four: Blossoming and Growing

During this stage of change, the focus is on continued growth. Here are some ideas to guide you in this period of change:

- *Check your bearings.* Are you in line with your needs, desires, and values? Or have you become distracted and lured off the path? What do you need to do to get on track and stay there? Consider where you need to head on the next leg of your journey to a better life. Let the seeds of your plan emerge now so that over the next few seasons they can germinate.

153

- *Write out your current options.* Note which ones provide the greatest opportunity for growth in the areas that are important to you. Cross off those that take you in tempting directions that are not in line with your principles, values, and general guidelines for living.
- *Confide in your closest friends.* How do they see your decisions and actions for change? Are they with you, or do they think you have strayed off the path that is best for you?

■ Stages of Change

One of the risks you need to take to be successful is to embrace change. We face some changes that we can't control. Many of us resist the idea of having to move to a different neighborhood, city, or school. But we can't let the fear of change prevent us from being successful. We have to learn how to manage the changes in our lives—to take advantage of the opportunities we have to make changes for the better.

We described the process of change in four stages: letting go, sticking to your plans, holding on tight, and blossoming and growing. Answer the following questions about each stage. But before you do, think a moment about a change that you feel would be good for you to make in your life, but one that would be difficult for you to make. It could be a behavior, a thought pattern, an attitude, a way of life. Consider a change that will help you toward your vision.

Got it? Okay. Answer these questions about that change that you have in mind.

■ Stage One: Letting Go

What are the things you will have to give up in order to make the change you want?

_____

_____

Will these things be hard to give up? If so, why?

_____

_____

How would you feel if you let go of them?

_____

_____

What would help you let go of them?

_____

_____

What would happen if you let go of them?

_____

_____

What would happen if you *didn't* let go of them?

_____

_____

■ Stage Two: Sticking to Your Plans

Now imagine that you have let go of the things you needed to make the change. You are now in the midst of making the change. How do you feel? Why?

_____

_____

If you're feeling anxious or are worrying about the change and whether you can do it, what will help you focus on the positive and keep going?

_____

_____

What tends to pull you down or makes you feel shaky in your decisions to change?

_____

_____

When are you most tempted to give up on a change, even if you think it's for the better?

_____

_____

What motivates you to continue on with a change, even if you're feeling a bit shaky or uncertain?

_____

_____

■ Stage Three: Holding on Tight

You've stuck to your plans so far. Good job! You're beginning to adapt to your change. But you're still experiencing ups and downs in this stage. How good are you at managing the ups and downs of change? Are you adaptable and flexible?

_____

_____

During this stage you often are moved from a passive to an active role in change, or from _thinking_ about change to actually _making change happen_ in your life. Do you have trouble going from thinking about doing something to actually doing it? If so, why?

_____

_____

You often make rapid, but at times erratic, progress in this stage. If you stumble or make a bad decision in your change, what do you do?

_____

_____

Why is it important to stay focused on your primary goals during this stage?

_____

_____

■ Stage Four: Blossoming and Growing

Congratulations! You've successfully made a change in your life. How does it feel having made that change?

_____

_____

How is your life better?

_____

_____

What other areas of growth or opportunities might open up as a result of the change you made?

_____

_____

Seeking Change

Some change is forced upon you by external circumstances. Other change you bring about yourself to create opportunities. Quite often these types of change are mixed.

> For instance, Phanedra was forced to make a change when her mother enrolled her in the after-school program. At first she had difficulty accepting the change, but then she decided to make the most of it. Had Phanedra not changed her approach to her new situation, she would not have succeeded. She was placed in the midst of new circumstances, but it wasn't until she decided to seek the good in that change that she began to flourish.

How you approach change is so crucial to your ability to adapt and to use change to learn and to improve your life. If you are to seek a better life than the one you have now, you have to *make your own changes* and not just wait for good things to happen to you. You have to stop just going along and getting along and start chasing your dreams and challenging life. That takes courage. Seeking and dealing with change, even positive change, requires self-control, patience, and perseverance. Change can emotionally overwhelm you so that your power to reason is diminished and your vision of a better life is clouded.

Remember the stage of change I described as "letting go"? If you can't let go of something, it's hard to seek change, even if you want it badly. It's like trying to drive with the parking brake on: You want to go but you're being held back.

I see this concept acted out sometimes on the playground a few blocks away from where I live. I see parents helping their children get started on a set of monkey bars on the playground. Young children often are afraid to let go with one hand to grab the next bar so they can go across the full length of the bars. But once they get the hang of it, they understand that, to move across the bars, they have to follow a process of holding on with one hand, letting go with the other, getting a grip on the next bar, and pulling themselves forward.

When they come to understand the process, they willingly make the changes necessary to move ahead. Now they see that change can be a *good* thing. It can bring them what they want. As Albert Einstein said, "The significant problems we face cannot be solved at the same level of thinking we were at when we created them." You can't always find the answers within your existing environment; sometimes you have to seek change in order to find answers.

> **I**f you are to seek a better life than the one you have now, you have to *make your own changes* and not just wait for good things to happen to you.

Changing for the Better

Remember Matt? He had started as a sophomore and junior on his basketball team, but as a senior his coach put him on the bench. Matt had a new role: He was sixth man, the spark plug off the bench who picked the team up when they were lagging, who filled in for younger starters.

Now, of course he preferred to start. But he accepted his new role. And he began to flourish in it. Midway through the season, the team began to click. Attitudes changed. The players were more aggressive and hungry; they hustled more; they were more selfless in their play. Each player began to do what he could to contribute to the team, rather than try to gain as much personal glory as he could. As disbelieving and upset as the players were at the beginning of the season, they were a much-improved team. The changes they had gone through were difficult. But they were definitely for the better.

> To be honest, about half the team was ready to walk about two weeks into practice. We didn't understand the changes that Coach Harding was bringing about, and we liked how we'd done things in the past. We all knew our roles—until Coach Harding came in.
>
> All I can say is, I'm glad we didn't walk. I wouldn't want to go through that kind of season every year—but we learned a lot. And we came to realize that Coach Harding was right. Once that started to click in, we didn't mind the changes so much.
>
> Gary, age 17, Matt's teammate

Why then do so many people treat any and every proposed change as if it were a deadly disease? Resistance to change is nearly as certain, and as inevitable, as change itself. Our society is always boiling with change: changing fashions, changing technology, changing moral principles, changing markets. It seems that change occurs more rapidly with each passing year. Think how things have changed in your life in the last three years. Such constant change is like an unrelenting and powerful wind or water current that can wear down trees and even rock.

The point is this: Change is happening all the time, both in the world at large and in your own private world. Those who adapt to change, meet the challenges that change brings with it, and accept change and see in it new opportunities to grow are the ones who find success. These people know how to manage change.

Managing Change

Sometimes even minor changes in your life can trigger strong feelings. Your car breaks down on the way to school one day. It puts you in a foul mood for that day and for the rest of the week you have to take a bus to school. You detest getting on the bus after experiencing the freedom of driving by yourself. Or during summer your best friend goes off to camp or on vacation; suddenly your daily routine is altered. You sulk around the house and scowl; you suddenly don't know what to do with yourself.

Bigger changes evoke even stronger emotions and feelings. Your parents get divorced. Your older sister has a baby. Your father loses his job. Your young nephew dies. Your older brother wins the lottery (that's the good news) and suddenly seems not to recognize you (that's the bad news). Such unexpected events carry with them intense feelings that may interfere with your ability to function.

Even outwardly positive changes such as a move to a nicer house can bring with it feelings of sadness and disorientation brought on by leaving the old neighborhood. Even though the new house might be nice, the satisfaction of moving in can be soured by such feelings, particularly if they are unanticipated. Such unexpected feelings can make us resent even positive change, unless we learn to deal with them. That is what *managing your response to change* is all about.

> I thought the guy was a creep, if you want to know the truth. I didn't want a step-dad. I had a real dad. Even if he wasn't living in our house anymore, I had a father. The thought of my stepfather moving into our house made me physically sick. I was really mad at my mom.
>
> Jessica, age 14

A key point in this chapter is that *just as change is natural, so are those feelings that accompany it.* Jessica is expressing her anger at her parents getting divorced, and at the changes that are resulting. There's nothing wrong with her feelings. But along with those feelings, she needs to learn how to manage that change to make it work for her.

Matt was not pleased with his new situation on the basketball team. He had loved being a starter. He felt proud of starting and loved playing lots of minutes. He was as upset as anyone when the new coach brought in such sweeping changes. But he knew that his feelings of anger and resentment were natural, so he did not fight the changes that caused them. He accepted his feelings without letting them affect his behavior. He effectively managed a change in his life and, as a result, he contributed more effectively to the team and experienced ultimately greater satisfaction as the team won its league championship in his senior year.

Taking Matt's cue, we need to learn how to manage change. In the next few pages we'll focus on three ways to do so: by controlling anger, developing patience, and handling stress. If you can do these three things, you're well on your way to managing change.

Controlling Your Anger

As with Matt's teammates, unexpected or unwelcome changes often trigger anger. Controlling that anger is extremely important. The anger is, in truth, fleeting, but the effects can be long-lasting and damaging.

Two of Matt's teammates were kicked off the team because they became openly hostile and rebellious toward the coach and could not control their anger. They could have benefited from the following five tips for controlling anger in times of change.

1. *Step back and look at the big picture.*

    Anger is a natural response. In times of danger or stress, anger triggers increased blood flow and the adrenaline prepares people for flight or fight. This emotion serves a purpose, but you want to make sure it serves *your* purpose. Are you directing your anger at the real source of your resentment? And even if you have the right target, are you hurting yourself? Don't sabotage yourself because of fleeting anger. Put the anger aside and assess the situation. If your anger is being vented in a self-destructive manner, find another way to vent it.

2. *Remove yourself from the scene of the crime.*

    If a change has triggered powerful feelings of anger and resentment, make a strategic retreat. Take that anger somewhere and let it vent on a run or through a punching bag (just make sure it's a bag and not a person!).

Use that energy; don't store it. But use it wisely, away from the situation that made you angry in the first place.

3. *Transform negative emotions to positive action.*

If you are angry with a teacher because that teacher doesn't see your potential, use that energy to excel in class and prove the teacher wrong. If you are angry at a friend who has betrayed a secret of yours, use the energy to become more trustworthy yourself. Don't be hurtful or vengeful; do something positive to ease your anger and to gain perspective.

4. *Talk it out.*

Talk with friends or family members who are not immediately involved in whatever is triggering your anger. Go somewhere away from the scene of the crime, and talk through your anger to avoid saying things or doing things that will only hurt you or your cause.

5. *Take stock of your options.*

Many times anger is the result of feeling trapped and robbed of opportunities, but in truth, your anger may be blinding you to the opportunities that await. It has been said that in times of change, people concentrate far too much on the door that has been closed, rather than looking for those that have been opened. Rather than being swept up emotionally, charge up mentally and consider what opportunities might have opened up by the change that has triggered your anger. Now is the time to act, not react.

Let's take an example: Your history teacher has just kicked you and a friend out of class for goofing off. In truth, you *weren't* goofing off; you were only marginally and unintentionally involved. The teacher, however, isn't listening to your pleas; he just orders you to go to the principal's office.

You could blow up at your friend or at the teacher. You could be angry for a long time at both of them and "show" the teacher by not working hard for him. But that would just hurt your grade.

The wiser choice is this: Take your anger out of the classroom with you. If you feel like it, run home after school to vent your anger; just don't vent it in unproductive ways within sight or hearing distance of the teacher. Talk it over with family or friends; tell them what really happened. And then determine to prove the teacher wrong; you're not a troublemaker or a goof-off. You're a student. Chances are he'll be watching you more closely in the next few classes, to make sure you've learned your lesson and don't goof off again. Use that extra attention to showcase your ability as a student. Show him where your head and your heart are. Turn that anger and a negative situation into something positive.

Developing Patience

As you know by now, mastering change is vital to the Success Process. A primary virtue needed in this mastery is that of patience. You cannot rush change; you have to allow it to unfold in the manner that is best suited to your nature. Patience is a very difficult virtue to acquire for many people.

You cannot shortcut your way through the change process. You need to *expect* that change will throw you off somewhat, that it will take adapting to. People who aren't very patient can give up on change before they derive the benefits from it. If you're like this, you're going through a lot of pain for nothing, because you're turning back before you get to the promised land. Expect bumps and jolts along the way and ride them through. The way you do that is with patience.

Let's say you're really interested in music, and you decide that you want to play in a band with some friends, or play in the school band. But you've never played an instrument before. You have your work cut out for you. You will have to change your daily routine, because you'll need to practice daily. And once the thrill of getting your own instrument wears off, and the reality of the work sets in, it won't be easy. For those of you who have played guitar, do you remember what it was like those first few weeks and months? Your fingertips can get so sore they crack and bleed. You probably never realized there were so many nerve endings in one tiny place! It takes patience to stick with learning something new, or changing behavior, or adapting to new circumstances. And if you are learning guitar and you give it up after three months, you have some sore fingers and a lot of wasted practice time to show for it.

> People who aren't very patient can give up on change before they derive the benefits from it.

Patience! Our culture is not very keen on patience. We want what we want, and we want it today, not tomorrow. The great technological advances we enjoy are part blessing, part curse. We're getting more and more accustomed to having everything at our fingertips, everything within moments. Microwave ovens, remote controls for televisions and other electronic equipment, and the Internet are just a few examples of speeding the process of getting what we want—usually while we sit down in an easy chair waiting (but not waiting long!) for it.

It's no wonder many people struggle with being patient. We want immediate solutions to problems, and immediate results, but we often aren't willing to put in the time or energy to get those solutions and results. If you want to get a step ahead of most people in taking on change and making it work for you, then develop patience. Don't be so quick to judge a change or give up on it (or on yourself). Good things don't always come quickly. Some change takes time. Give it the time it needs, and you may be quite surprised—and pleased—with the results.

Handling the Stress of Change

Realize that when you make a change in your life, you will experience conflicting feelings. It is only natural, just as change itself is natural. The process of change can be stressful, even when the changes are for the better. You need a game plan for handling that stress. Here are five tips for dealing with the stress of change.

1. *Stay focused on your dream for a better life.*

   Sure, you may hit hard times when you make a change. Your friends may criticize you. You may doubt yourself. It may be exhausting to do all that is required to get to the next level of achievement or preparation. I never said it would be easy. But you can ease some of the stress by not focusing on *how hard it is.* Instead, keep in mind *how much better it will be* when you have completed this change.

2. *Stay true to your principles and beliefs.*

   Stress can be triggered when you do things that go against your beliefs and values. The process of change can test those basic beliefs and, occasionally, you may find that you have compromised your beliefs. You may find yourself being untruthful or in other situations that you would not normally have to contend with. This is stressful because you are violating your own rules. To avoid this stress, do your best to stay within your normal guidelines for behavior. Be aware that temporarily abandoning those guidelines will have serious and stressful consequences.

3. *Give yourself a break.*

   Understand that stress comes with change and compensate for that by giving yourself a break. Take time out from the usual routine to reduce stress and mental fatigue. Do things that recharge you emotionally, physically, intellectually, and spiritually. Stress is taking energy from you; you need to renew that energy.

4. *Unload your calendar.*

   This is not a time to take on more projects or challenges that will add to your stress load. Don't burn the candle at both ends; take time to relax. When you are undergoing change in one part of your life, try to keep the other areas of your life under control. Take on no more than one major stressor at a time, if possible. Put off nonessential changes for a later time.

163

5. *Put out your distress signals.*

Far too many people are unwilling to ask for help when they're stressed. Why have friends and family if you can't lean on them in hard times? I take it as a compliment when friends come to me when they need support. It makes me feel needed and valuable in their lives. You don't want to overdo it, but in critical times, put out the signal that you need some support.

TEENS CAN MAKE IT HAPPEN

■ Changing Your Way of Thinking

Three keys to adapting to change are to control your anger, develop patience, and handle stress. Change brings with it a wealth of emotions; it can at times be like a roller coaster ride. Answer the following questions to examine how well you adapt to change and how anger, patience, and stress affect your ability to change.

Think about a recent change in your life, whether it was a move to a new home, a change in your classes or extracurricular activities, a change in a personal relationship.

Write down the change that occurred. _____

_____.

Note how you felt about the change.
The things I liked about the change were: _____

_____.

The things I didn't like about the change were: _____

_____.

Were you surprised by those emotions?

_____

_____

Overall, do you now regard the change as a positive or as a negative experience?

_____

_____

Based on how things turned out, do any of the fears, concerns, or negative emotions that you experienced now seem justified?

_____

_____

Do you think you could have managed your response to the change better?

_____

_____

■ Anger, Patience, and Stress

What types of change might make you angry?

_____

_____

Why?

_____

_____

Has anger ever negatively affected how you adapted to what turned out to be a positive change in your life?

_____

_____

What can you do to turn anger into something positive when you face your next big change?

_____

_____

Are you normally a patient person when it comes to important things, or do you tend to give up on things too early?

_____

_____

What types of things are you willing to be patient for?

_____

_____

How can patience help you achieve your goals?

_____

_____

Think of a time when you were stressed with a big change going on in your life. What was your response to that change?

_____

_____

If you could go back and do things differently, would you respond differently to that change? How?

_____

_____

What are ways that you can unload stress and relax?

_____

_____

There's no doubt about it—change is a constant in our lives. By learning to let go of things and sticking to your plan, you can begin to make change work for you. Learning how to control your anger, develop patience, and handle stress are three keys that will help you adapt to change and use it for your own good.

One important way to handle stress is to ask for help from others, rather than carrying the burden alone. Support from others is a key to your success; no one truly makes it on his or her own. What you need to do is build your own "dream team." We'll explore how to do that in the next chapter.

8 Build Your Dream Team

Self-realization would not be achieved one by one, but all together or not at all.

W. E. B. Du Bois

Turning your dream into reality doesn't happen easily. Many people think they can, or *should,* try to go it alone as they pursue their dreams and goals. The truth is, if you want meaningful, long-term success, you need others to help you achieve it.

Success comes not only through your own efforts, but through the assistance, guidance, and encouragement from many others. It doesn't matter whether you're talking about small or personal success, or victories where the whole world takes notice.

Would Neil Armstrong have walked on the moon in 1969 without the direct support of hundreds of people from NASA? Did John Elway win a Super Bowl with the Denver Broncos on his own? Are advances in science and medicine and technology made by one person without relying heavily on past discoveries? Astronauts, athletes, scientists, and doctors don't operate within a vacuum, totally relying on their own wisdom and strength and ingenuity. In fact, the more they rely on successful and skillful people around them, the more successful they become.

This is true in much smaller scales and in different arenas, too. Thousands of people rely on Alcoholics Anonymous and similar organizations to get over addictions and learn different behaviors. To these people, taking such a step is the most important step they can take to better their lives, and they couldn't do it without the support of others. And there are numerous organizations for younger people—Junior Achievement, Boy Scouts, Girl Scouts, and on and on—where success comes from a true team effort.

Or take another example: If you want to learn how to play the saxophone, you can try to teach yourself, but you'll do much better if you hook up with a good instructor. No matter what the endeavor, you'll find that goals are easier to achieve through the help of others. It may sound romantic to "go it alone," but it is not an effective way to approach the Success Process. In fact, I believe that *no one* makes it alone; building and maintaining mutually supportive relationships is *essential* if you are to successfully pursue a meaningful life.

In this chapter we'll explore three essential areas in considering how to build the types of relationships that can help you realize your dreams. We'll look at how to

- Use teamwork to reach goals,
- Build trust, and
- Grow your support team.

Using Teamwork to Reach Goals

A key element of the Success Process is building relationships with people who care about you and believe in your goals as you grow and expand the possibilities for your life. Having relationships that strengthen you is vital. How many people do you know who have been urged on to succeed and to develop their talents by those people around them? I know many, many people like that. I also know people who have had difficulty building better lives for themselves because they didn't have anyone in their corner cheering them on, advising them, and helping them to get through the hard times.

In my senior year at Middle Township High School, our basketball team went all the way to the state finals, even though we were a very small school. We did so well not because we had a lot of great individual players, but because we had a great *team*. There were other teams with more talented players; in fact, some of them had too much talent. On some teams loaded with good players, everybody wants to be a star, rather than trying to fit in with the other players.

We had a group of guys who were willing to do what was good for the team, rather than worrying about their individual statistics and achievements. Each of us trusted the other to do what was good for the team as a whole. Each of us worked to earn that trust in order to prove that we deserved to be part of the team. As a result, we achieved more *together* than we ever would have achieved if we each had played merely for personal glory. We were bound together by mutual trust and respect and common goals, so we were not only a basketball team; each of us was part of the *support team* for the other players.

Think in terms of your own experience. Have you accomplished your proudest achievements entirely on your own, or through the support and help and encouragement of others? Team sports is an obvious example of the teamwork it takes to reach goals, but for every achievement there is some type of support system behind it. And this support system works both ways—that is, at times you will need that support and help for yourself; at other times you will be supporting and helping others. That's what teamwork is about: banding together to help each other reach goals. Whether you realize it or not, you are part of a team—or more likely, several loose-knit teams.

Being Part of a Team

Examples of formal teams are found in high schools not only in sports, but in music (bands and groups), education (various types of clubs), and social groups. We have lots of opportunities to be part of informal teams, beginning with our families and extending to our friends, to our churches and synagogues, and beyond.

The reality is we all are parts of many types of teams, some formal, others informal. Forming and maintaining supportive, positive relationships is not only essential to our success, it is also one of the most enjoyable and rewarding parts of life. We all need a team behind us to share in our victories and to help us overcome our defeats. In every aspect of life, whether it is in the home, at school, or in the community, we need people who share our vision for a better life.

I had studied really hard for my geometry test. And I got a C-. I was so bummed, let me tell you. I had decided I was going to work really hard at my grades, and I wanted to get nothing lower than a B.

I was in this really bad mood for the whole day. Then Angie—she's my best friend—she says, "You know, it's not the end of the world, you can do better next time." We hung out together after school for a while and I began to feel better. She has this way of making me feel good about myself. I tell you, sometimes I don't know what I'd do without friends like her.

Shari, age 15

Understanding Our Heritage of Teamwork

Teamwork is hardly a new concept in helping people achieve better lives. The cathedrals of medieval Europe are surely among the most striking examples of the power of human cooperation, but there are many others, from the Roman aqueducts to the Great Wall of China.

That teamwork exists today in times of crises, when we come together regardless of our differences. Earthquakes, fires, mudslides, hurricanes, tornadoes, plane crashes, and other disasters create chaos that often inspires heroic, cooperative efforts of people from different backgrounds. Teams of scientists, engineers, medical personnel, social workers, and all kinds of volunteers respond to crises, with examples ranging from nuclear disaster in Chernobyl in 1986 to more recent examples such as the crises in war-torn Rwanda and Bosnia in the 1990s.

Closer to home, prison inmates, who are generally regarded as the most antisocial of people, have volunteered to help fight flooding in the Midwest in recent years. The townspeople who have benefited from their labors, and often worked alongside them, have marveled at the transformations that occur in these outcasts when they are thrown into a cooperative effort for the good of others.

So what does this mean for you? It means you look to help others when they need help, and you look to call on others for help when you need it. That may mean you have to swallow your pride to ask for help. That may make you uncomfortable. Maybe you're a loner—whether by choice or not—and you can't imagine teaming up with others in any way that can be meaningful.

It won't be meaningful if you don't give it a chance. But if you really want

> We all need a team behind us to share in our victories and to help us overcome our defeats.

TEENS CAN MAKE IT HAPPEN

to achieve your goals, you have to build a dream team to help you. You have to forge positive partnerships.

Forging Positive Partnerships

So how do you choose your dream team wisely? Successful teams—whether formal or informal, whether a group of twenty or of two—have these five characteristics in common:

1. They are committed to a common goal.
2. They share common values and expectations.
3. They play complementary roles.
4. They have a plan for confronting and solving problems.
5. They have a plan for evaluating progress.

Let's take a closer look at each characteristic.

Common Goals. The first key is for all on the "team" to agree on goals. If you don't share the same goals, it's impossible to decide how to work together to achieve them. Listen to this testimony:

> My brother and I argued for about an hour, back and forth, back and forth, until suddenly I just sort of sat back and smiled. This just made him all the madder. "What's so funny?" he asked. I said, "We're arguing for the same thing. We want the same thing. We just want Mom to be happy, that's all." Mom had just got re-married and we didn't agree on whether she should have or not. But we both wanted the same thing: We wanted her to be happy. After that we calmed down a little.
>
> Steve, age 16

Let's look at some other situations. If your goal is to really focus on improving your grades this semester, you don't hang out with dropouts. If you want to do well on the track team next spring, you aren't going to help your cause by hanging out with a group who smokes and eats poorly and gets no exercise.

Make sure that your support team understands your goals. If your education plans include getting an advanced degree, you aren't going to get much support or understanding from those who don't care about education. If you have a strong social conscience and want to work for various social causes, you won't enlist much help from those who don't share those goals. If you want to campaign for

171

student council, your campaign won't be helped by friends who think that such councils are a joke.

Sharing common goals is at the center of positive relationships. Rather than wasting energy trying to explain your goals or to win people over, you can *gain* energy from like-minded people who not only understand your goals, but feel the same way about them that you do. Sharing common goals can also act as glue when trouble arises, because you know that you are after the same thing. It can hold teams together when they encounter problems. We'll talk more about this in a moment.

Common values and expectations. People on winning teams share common expectations about how everyone on the team should behave, including agreeing on what role each member is expected to play. This goes for any team you put together, too. Your family and friends might help you reach personal goals. Teachers and counselors can help you reach education goals. Each person contributes something of value to the effort. Each one shares the core values that are behind the effort, and each one knows the role he or she can play to help you achieve your goal.

Sharing common goals is at the center of positive relationships.

In musical groups, direction for the team is provided by the musical score. On your team, you and the team members set the direction. You agree upon expected behavior based upon the group's values. Those who hold greatly differing values are likely to have very different ideas about appropriate behavior in the relationship and won't provide much lasting support.

For example, let's say you and your best friend from childhood were just that—best friends—in part because you shared the same values. But in the past few years your friend has taken a path down a road that embraces different values: He or she is now indulging in alcohol, drugs, and other risky behavior. Your friend's values are no longer your values. And the expectations your friend has—namely that you take part in things you want no part of—have resulted in a disagreement between you and this lifelong friend that has loosened the bonds of the friendship. Even if you remain friends with this person, you will not include him or her in your support team, because you no longer share the same values and expectations and thus will receive little support from this friend.

On the other hand, if this friend were caught up in a lifestyle that he or she didn't value and wanted to change, you could turn out to be a very important member of your friend's team. The key is in the values. While no two people agree on every issue, it's hard to maintain a lasting, supportive relationship when the people involved have substantially differing values.

Complementary roles. Musicians must decide which instrument each will play and which part the vocalists will sing. So, too, people involved in successful partnerships know what part each will play in achieving their mutually agreed-upon goals.

Clarity about roles is essential. It gives your team members the information they need about how they fit into the game plan, what they can expect from each other, and how their roles interact. If each person's role is not clearly defined, conflict is likely.

For instance, let's say that no one in your family has graduated from college before, but you have plans to not only graduate from college but to perhaps attain an advanced degree. Members of your support team can and should play distinct roles. For example:

- Your family offers encouragement.
- Your teachers help shape your educational goals.
- Your career counselor guides you in career and college choices.
- A friend might tutor you (or you might be involved in a study group with friends with similar goals).
- A family acquaintance or a mentor who is in the field you are interested in offers guidance and insight.
- Your parents, in addition to offering encouragement and emotional support, also provide financial support and apply for financial aid to help you reach your goal.
- A few close friends offer emotional support and encouragement.

Everyone plays a distinct part, and together the support, guidance, and encouragement offered is significant.

Confronting and solving problems. Conflict is a part of life. Even on the closest of teams disagreements will occur. You need to find ways to resolve conflicts so that the team always moves forward rather than getting hung up on internal problems. Can you imagine a musical performance in which members of the band stop playing because they can't agree on how to interpret a song? How about a basketball team so torn apart by jealousies and misunderstandings that it can't compete?

If you're part of a group or team that has a conflict it cannot solve, one of two things happens: You hobble along in a crippled state, achieving far less than you reasonably should, or you disband altogether. In fact, part of the strength of a healthy team is that it can solve problems and achieve more together when it works through the hard times.

173

For instance, in keeping with the last example, let's say your desires to graduate from college are meeting with opposition from your mother. She is not against higher education, but she is concerned about the family's financial situation and can't see how this new financial burden can be added. She is already working two part-time jobs as it is, your father is working a full-time job, and they are barely making ends meet. In a healthy situation, you can confront and solve the problem following these six steps.

1. *Define the problem.*

    The first step in resolving conflict is to decide together what the problem is. That means you identify areas of disagreement and agreement. In this case the problem is you want to go to college; while your mother agrees this is a worthy goal, she feels that the family cannot afford the financial burden.

2. *Diagnose the causes.*

    Next, it is important to understand what led to the conflict. Conflict can be caused by many things, including actions or events, comments or rumors of comments made, or conflicting goals. Sometimes it helps to bring in a neutral third party to help sort through conflicting information. The cause of the conflict here is the worry about the finances.

3. *Generate possible solutions.*

    Identify possible resolutions of the conflict and actions each person can take to achieve the resolution. For instance, you and your mother can look into various grants and forms of financial aid available, and your parents can assess the family budget to see if money could be set apart to either begin or increase an already existing budget for education. Other possible solutions would be to go to a junior college for two years before transferring to a more expensive four-year college or university, or to go to school part-time and work part-time.

4. *Decide on a mutually acceptable solution.*

    Consider the effects of various solutions and select the option most acceptable to the parties. In this case, perhaps you decide on attending a reputable junior college while working part-time and applying for scholarships and grants to be used when you transfer to a four-year college.

5. *Implement the solution.*

    Once the parties involved have agreed on a solution, they should all be involved in implementing it. Continuing our example, you would attend junior college, work part-time, and apply for scholarships and grants at the appropriate time.

6. *Evaluate the results.*

All parties involved should evaluate how well the solution solved the problem. If it didn't solve the problem, seek another solution. In this case, you would evaluate the usefulness of the junior college in terms of it helping you meet your educational goals, and of your success in raising enough money and financial aid to later transfer to a four-year college.

Evaluating progress. Successful teams have ways to evaluate how much progress they are making. Teammates agree upon the goal itself, and upon ways to evaluate progress, so that progress can be measured.

Some goals are simple and clear-cut. For most teams in sports, the goal is to win the game. The evaluation of their progress is simple: If they win they have reached their immediate goal and are advancing toward their long-term goal; if they lose they are not making progress.

But even most sports teams have other, smaller goals that, if reached, will help them toward their overall goal of winning. A football team may have goals of controlling the clock, eating up yards on the ground, and wearing down their opponent in the process. A basketball team might have a goal of controlling the backboards, gaining more rebounds than the opponent. The teams might have several smaller goals related directly to performance. Then, at the end of the game, if they lost, they can look at their performance goals and see where they fell short, as opposed to knowing that they simply scored fewer points.

Other goals are not so simple or clear-cut and therefore can be more difficult to evaluate. That's all the more reason to agree upon measurable checkpoints along the way.

Part of the strength of a healthy team is that it can solve problems and achieve more together when it works through the hard times.

Father:	So how's your paper coming?
Son:	My what?
Father:	Your paper. For American History.
Son:	Oh. Umm . . . I'm still working on it.
Father:	When's it due?
Son:	Umm . . . tomorrow.
Father:	And how far along are you?
Son:	Well, I've, uh, got all the stuff together and everything . . . I just have to write it now.
Father:	In other words, you haven't started.

Son:	Well, not the writing part, no. But I've got it all up here [taps his head].
Father:	What did I tell you about setting some checkpoints along the way? We talked about this. You do the research, write an outline, write a first draft, and then revise the paper. How do you expect to do that all in one night?
Son:	Umm . . . I wasn't planning on sleeping much.

That student would surely have benefited from having some checkpoints along the way, as his father suggested!

When you undertake this five-step process to forge positive relationships—committing to a common goal, sharing common values and expectations, playing complementary roles, confronting and solving problems, and evaluating progress—you also are taking a step toward another important aspect of building your dream team: building trust. After you complete the following worksheet, we'll look at ways to build trust.

■ Teaming Up to Win

Relationships that are positive and make you stronger are critical to your ability to achieve your goals. Some partnerships are more successful than others. Identify a person who has had a positive influence on you in your pursuit of a goal.

Your positive teammate was:

_____

Identify one thing that worked well in this relationship. Possible responses might include:

- We got along well.
- My teammate was very supportive.
- We communicated well.
- We were always able to solve problems.
- We agreed on what we should do and how we were going to do it.
- We trusted each other completely.
- We agreed on what was most important.

_____

_____

Identify one thing that did not work well in a different relationship. Possible responses might be:

- We couldn't agree on what to do.
- We had very different methods.
- I didn't trust this teammate.
- I had to do all the work.
- We didn't communicate very well.

_____

_____

Think of a time when you pursued a goal. It could be the goal in question above, or it could be a different goal. Consider the teammate or teammates who were on your team for this goal. Assess how successful you were in the five key characteristics of forging positive partnerships by answering the following questions.

Was everyone on the team committed to the same goal? If not, why not?

_____

_____

If some people were not committed to the same goal, what was the result?

_____

_____

Did everyone on the team share common values and expectations?

_____

_____

If not, what was the result of that conflict?

_____

_____

Did each person know his or her role on the team?

_____

_____

If not, did conflict result from this confusion?

_____

_____

Was the team good at problem solving?

_____

_____

Did your team have a way to evaluate your progress toward the goal?

_____

_____

If not, how would a way to evaluate have helped you?

_____

_____

Building Trust

So you want the support and encouragement of others around you, but no one is there for you? That could be the case for a lot of reasons: Perhaps you're not very open with other people, and they don't know you well enough to know where you need help. Maybe you are good at asking for help but never bother to return the favor when asked. Or maybe others see in you an attitude of "I don't care" or "I don't need anybody's help," and if *you* don't care, they surely won't. Or perhaps it's because you haven't proven yourself trustworthy. You won't be able to build much of a support team if you gossip behind your friends' backs, or take things from them, or don't keep your word.

Trust is not easily earned. Just look around you. How many people do you truly trust with your possessions, or to protect your privacy, or keep a secret, or to tell you the truth no matter what? The list probably isn't too long.

Real trust is established over time, through shared experiences and a pattern of reliability. The process begins in childhood. Although a child may be blindly trusting early on, even toddlers become wary of family members who prove to be unreliable or hurtful. If a child learns early on that his own parents and siblings cannot be trusted, odds are he will have difficulty establishing trusting relationships or being trustworthy himself, for the rest of his life.

And there's a difference between *acting* or *appearing* trustworthy and *being* trustworthy:

- Jamie's reputation has been smeared and Susan, her friend, stands up for her while eating with her in the school cafeteria. But then after school, when Jamie isn't around, Susan listens to a group gossiping about Jamie and then adds gossip of her own.
- Derreck has been challenged to a fight by a classmate with a mean reputation. Three of Derreck's friends are outraged by this and say they will be there to back him up. Thus bolstered by his friends' vows, Derreck shows up at the appointed time and finds himself facing the bully alone. His friends apparently realized they had other things to do.

179

If you want to appear trustworthy, *be* trustworthy. You can't fake trustworthiness. Oh, you may fool a few people for a short period of time, but not for long. Appearances will only get you so far. Think in terms of your own experience: Whom do you trust with truly important information? Those who look like they might be trustworthy? Or those who have actually *been* trustworthy?

I told Danielle and Jackie a pretty deep secret—and I sort of wished I hadn't told Jackie. She has this reputation for talking a lot, you know. Not bad stuff, but she just gossips a lot. So anyway I swore them both to secrecy, and they promised they wouldn't tell.

Then I found out that word had gotten out. Someone had told my secret. I was so mad! And hurt. I avoided Jackie for a while. Finally I went up to her and asked her how come she told. She said she didn't tell anyone. I didn't believe her. But then another friend came up and said that she'd heard Danielle tell my secret after school. I couldn't believe it! I thought Danielle was the one I could trust.

Sarah, age 17

There are all sorts of books that tell you how to appear trustworthy and sympathetic and honest, but in reality, having good character is the only way to earn the lasting trust and support of others. You don't just go out and buy good character. Nor do you develop it overnight. Again, it comes with a pattern of behavior, a way of living your life by certain rules based on age-old principles as basic and as enduring as the Golden Rule.

There is risk involved in trusting others. Not all relationships involve the same degree of trust, but trust is the key to building relationships and support teams. Trusting others can have both positive and negative consequences, and those consequences depend on how your team members respond to situations as you progress along the Success Process. You have to be able to read others' motives. Everyone has an agenda, a personal goal that may or may not be compatible with yours. You can't expect others to give your concerns and goals priority over theirs. The key is to find people whose goals are *compatible* with yours.

Inspiring Trust in Others

Behaving in a trustworthy manner, as opposed to just talking a good game, is important in building trust. There are other ways to inspire others to trust you, too. Here are eleven character traits that inspire trust.

1. *Do what you say you will do.*

   If you say you will meet with someone to study after school, be there at the appointed time. If you say you will back someone up in some issue, back that person up. If you say you will help a friend run a campaign for student council, follow through.

It's amazing how many people fail to live up to their promises, but still expect people to trust them. Again, you may fool some people for a while, but eventually the crowds will thin, and you'll be left making false promises to thin air. On the other hand, if you consistently live up to the expectations that you create, you may have to build an arena to accommodate the crowds that want to line up on your side.

When your actions follow your words, you don't have to work to impress people or to win them over. In time, they will see the strength of your character and line up to be on your support team. If you consistently do not make good on your word, however, you will be one of those people who specializes in short-term friendships, skipping from person to person, crowd to crowd, as people grow weary of your deceptions and unreliability.

2. *Listen without judgment.*

If a friend says she has something to tell you, and she seems shameful or fearful, listen without judging her. There is no greater favor you can do for someone than to be a devoted and trusted listener. Not an adviser or counselor, simply a listener. Give your friend your full attention and allow her to state the situation or express her emotions. Don't interrupt, don't be distracted, and don't try to give her a solution while she is talking. Let her talk without her fearing what your thoughts are on the matter.

> It's amazing how many people fail to live up to their promises, but still expect people to trust them.

3. *Be there.*

The importance of being there cannot be overstated. A friend told me that he recently filled in for a neighbor couple who had to leave town on the night of their son's school recital. He knew this boy, a second grader, fairly well, but had not spent a great deal of time alone with him. He did know, however, that it was important for the boy to have a familiar face in the crowd. The boy didn't say much on the way to the recital, and he didn't appear to care that this fellow was going to watch him perform. But when he took the stage, the first thing that boy did was scan the crowd for his neighbor's face. When he saw it, he lit up. The neighbor was where he said he would be. He knew how important it would be to the boy. That says more about the character of this neighbor than any claims he might make.

4. *Pay what you owe when it is due.*

This sounds almost revolutionary in a time of credit cards and delayed payment plans, but in personal transactions there is nothing that builds trust faster than paying debts promptly. This refers not only to money, but to your word and to giving back what you owe in relationships.

This is especially important in personal relationships, where it can be easy to take advantage of friends without really meaning to. Many star quarterbacks in the National Football League give their offensive linemen meaningful gifts, because the quarterbacks recognize the very real support that the linemen offer. Take a hint and do likewise with your own support team—not with gifts that cost money, but by returning the support that you receive. It's those around you who offer you the most support that are often easiest to overlook. Look for ways to give back to those who are giving to you.

5. *Act honorably even when tempted or criticized.*

It is easy to be an honorable person if there is no temptation, or if your honor is never challenged. But how honorable would you be if you had access to test answers or if you were unfairly criticized by someone who had the knack for getting your goat? Perhaps you know people in school who cheat regularly and get away with it. Likely you would never trust these people in a critical situation because their honor runs no deeper than a scratch. The most important thing is to be honest with yourself first. Are you comfortable with your own integrity? It is vital to demonstrate integrity, to stand up for your beliefs, and to resist pressure to do what you know to be wrong.

6. *Tell the truth about yourself and others.*

Some people seem to be addicted to gossiping, spreading rumors, and outright lying. When you hear someone say something that you know isn't true, what happens? Their credibility with you is shot. You don't know if you can believe anything else they say, and you may wonder what they say about you when you're not around.

Telling the truth is fundamental to being trustworthy. I recently read a report that said lying on résumés is so widespread today that many employers take it for granted. I don't understand this at all. How can an employer trust someone who has lied about something so important as his or her education and experience? Similarly, would you trust a student you know has lied to a teacher?

7. *Guard what is entrusted to you.*

In trusting relationships, people share their greatest fears or most embarrassing moments because they trust each other. To do this with someone you do not know well is to expose yourself to criticism or rejection. I read recently of a high school boy who told his most trusted friend a secret. It was an extremely private matter, but this friend did not guard it as he should have. He told someone else, and within a few days, the boy's secret was out not only in the high school, but throughout the community. As a result, he was taunted and even threatened and, eventually, he had to leave the high school one year before graduation, all because his friend had betrayed his trust.

8. *Be a source of strength.*

If you want to have people to lean on in your troubled times, you have to be a source of strength for them when they are in need. No one is strong all the time, and even the weakest of us can provide support to those who trust and rely on us.

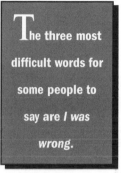

The three most difficult words for some people to say are *I was wrong.*

9. *Acknowledge your mistakes.*

The person who is willing to admit mistakes and imperfections is more likely to inspire confidence than one who never acknowledges being wrong or having weaknesses. Why? Because we all make mistakes and we all *know* we make mistakes. But many people go to great lengths to pretend they never make mistakes. The three most difficult words for some people to say are *I was wrong.* Who do you trust more, the person who always has an answer or an excuse, or the one who acknowledges his or her limits and errors?

10. *Help others without looking for praise or payment.*

Help people without seeking something in return. If you're helping a younger kid learn math theorems because you want to go out with his older sister, chances are the girl is going to see right through you. If, however, you take a genuine interest in the younger boy and truly offer to help him, chances are the girl is going to see something very good in you—and who knows? It may inspire her to want to go out with you. Help others without looking for rewards, and the rewards will probably find you anyway.

11. *Put the welfare of others before your own.*

To engender trust, show that you are as concerned about other people as you are about yourself. When other people know you have their best interests at heart, they'll trust you in the deepest matters, because few people place the well-being of others ahead of, or even on a par with, their own well-being.

■ Whom Do You Trust?

Make a list of the people on your team, those whom you trust to guard prized possessions, protect your privacy, keep a secret, and tell the truth no matter what. Next to each name, write down what makes each of them trustworthy.

_____ _____

_____ _____

_____ _____

_____ _____

Now, write down the names of people who might trust *you* in similar situations and what characteristics *you* have that make you trustworthy to each of them.

_____ _____

_____ _____

_____ _____

_____ _____

Are the same names on both lists?

_____

How hard was it to figure out what it is about another person that results in your trusting him or her?

_____

_____

What about identifying your own characteristics that result in others trusting you—was that hard to do, and how did it make you feel?

_____

_____

On a scale of 1 to 10, with 1 being very poor, 5 being average, and 10 being excellent, rate yourself on the eleven traits that inspire trust.

1. You do what you say you will do. _____
2. You listen without judgment. _____
3. You are there for your friends. _____

4. You pay what you owe—be it money, your word,
   whatever you owe others—when it is due. _____

5. You act honorably even when tempted or criticized. _____

6. You tell the truth about yourself and others. _____

7. You guard what is entrusted to you. _____

8. You are a source of strength for others when they need you. _____

9. You acknowledge your mistakes. _____

10. You help others without looking for praise or payment. _____

11. You put others' welfare before your own. _____

Score:

11–55	Poor
56–77	Average
78–88	Good
89–110	Excellent

Walking the Walk

You can talk a good game, but if you don't walk the walk, you'll find pretty soon that you're walking alone; because people won't trust you. Friends may hang around when matters aren't serious, but when the going gets tough, and trust becomes crucial, if you haven't proven yourself trustworthy, you won't have the support you need when you need it most.

Teammates practice and play together to build trust. Soldiers are trained together as combat units in order to build trust. Romantic relationships begin with dating and getting to know each other. Friendships begin with conversations and the sharing of mutual interests. Trust is important in any relationship, and it usually takes awhile to establish. Trust holds a relationship together over the long term. But it can be fragile and must be maintained and never taken for granted.

185

I guess I didn't realize how important it was to Jenny for me to be at her play. I told her I'd be there but then Mark asked me to go to a concert with him and I've been wanting to go out with him forever. I figured she would understand because she knew I was wanting to go out with Mark. But Jenny was so nervous about the play—it was her first big role—and I guess she needed my support. Now it's like she's real cool to me. It's not that she doesn't talk to me, but it's not the same.

Melinda, age 18

You establish trust by keeping your actions consistent with your words. You have to live it to earn it; you can't just say it. That is why the slow building of trust is so important to relationships. When you are building a support team, be patient in choosing your partners. Place as much trust in them as they have proven worthy of.

> When you walk the walk of trust and come through for others, you are building your own safety net, because people will be more likely to reciprocate.

Successful relationships are based upon trust and a shared sense that you can depend on each other even in hard times. Trust is knowing that your teammate has the required strength of character, sense of honor and truthfulness, and abilities to support you. Trust is knowing that people will come through for you when they say they will.

When you walk the walk of trust and come through for others, you are building your own safety net, because people will be more likely to reciprocate. You know that if you stumble, there will be someone there you trust to at least cushion your fall and help you back up.

Talking the Talk

Trust begins with good communication. If someone is difficult to talk with, if they don't listen to you or respond to you, the relationship probably isn't going anywhere. But relationships click when communication is good. For instance, you might hear it played out this way after a football game. The quarterback threw the winning touchdown pass to a receiver who broke his pattern to get free.

"How did you know Eddie was going to break his route?"

"Well, I saw he was covered and all my other receivers were covered, so . . ."

"But you threw the ball to the outside just *before* he broke to the outside. He was still running toward the middle of the field when you threw the pass *away from* him."

"He gave me this nod, toward the sideline. We don't break our patterns often, but I knew he meant he was going to go outside."

"You saw him nod?"

"We'd worked on it before. I knew what he meant."

In other words, they're on the same wavelength. This is important in all kinds of situations. Good communication is especially vital in building trusting relationships. Relationships deepen or fall apart based upon the quality of communication. Inevitably, there will be misunderstanding and miscommunications in almost any relationship, but there are ways to minimize those problems and to heighten your communications skills, which are sometimes called "interpersonal" skills.

Take this quick quiz. Fill in the blank:

_____ percent of how we communicate with others is through *nonverbal* communication—facial expressions, body language, and in the way we act.

a. 10 percent
b. 20 percent
c. 40 percent
d. 70 percent

> If you said "d"—70 percent—you are right. Communication gets jumbled when our nonverbal messages don't match our verbal messages. If you feel like other people are always misinterpreting you, then check your body language. It may be communicating something very different from your verbal message.

If actors in a play are working from different scripts, no one on stage or in the audience will understand the message. To help you stay on the same page with members of your support team, you need to work at effective communication. Sports teams and acting groups practice, practice, practice to sharpen communication between members.

Many people who think they are good communicators are not. Think about people whom you regard to be good leaders, whether it is a prominent national figure or someone within your own circle of friends. I'll bet that among the things each of those leaders has in common is the ability to communicate well, whether in writing, in one-on-one conversation, or when speaking to a group.

It may seem ironic, but as the world moves more and more to technology and electronic communication, the power to communicate well is increasingly valued. If you can't state your ideas well, it does you no good to have e-mail at your fingertips. No amount of high-tech equipment can mask poor communication skills. Technology has given us the ability to communicate instantaneously with people throughout the world. It is breaking down the boundaries that have historically separated us. It is hastening the development of a global village in which we are in constant and immediate reach of almost anyone anyplace in the world.

Growing Your Support Team

Relationships require good communication and they also require maintenance. If you take them for granted, they will wither and die. If you

abuse them, they will fall apart. To build trusting, supportive relationships, keep these five tips in mind. A few of these tips reinforce what you learned earlier about teamwork.

1. *Be the host, not the guest, in the relationship.*

A host is concerned about the guest's needs, interests, and point of view. If you're in a relationship where everything is "me, me, me," where the only needs you're concerned about are your own, then the relationship won't last long. Be attentive to the people who are part of your support team. Be there for them as much as you expect them to be there for you. Build trust by showing that you want to be an active force in that person's life.

2. *Pay attention to the details.*

A couple I know visited the home of a famous person not long ago. The host wined and dined my friends graciously, but what impressed my friends the most was the little things that this host did. "She personally put together a tray of goodies for our nightstand and saw to it that we had comfortable pillows," my friends reported. "She seemed to take a great deal of pride and interest in being a good host." It is the little things that often make the greatest impression; when you are building a trusting relationship, attention to the details can mean a lot. Remember special occasions and birthdays. Be alert to events and changes in the other person's life. Do so because you are truly involved and interested, because that is the only way to build trust.

3. *Honor all commitments, big and small, spoken and unspoken.*

Few things can build or tear down trust as quickly as keeping, or failing to keep, commitments. If you intend to build a trusting relationship with someone, be there when you say you will be there. Be prepared to honor the unspoken commitments. When my father died recently, the people I trust and depend on the most stepped forward. I did not have to ask for their support; there was no spoken commitment that they would be there for me in times of sadness in my life, but I knew they would be there and they were. Those people have made a commitment to our relationship that is based on far more than their own self-interests.

4. *Live up to your own expectations.*

Have you ever known someone who expected others to live by rules and principles that he or she openly ignored? That is what I am referring to when I say that you should live up to your own expectations. You cannot expect people to invest more in you than you are willing to invest in them. If you don't remember their birthdays, don't expect them to send a cake for yours. If you don't show up to celebrate their victories and successes or to console them in their setbacks, don't expect them to rush to your side on those occasions. If you expect members of your team to live with integrity, you had better be a model of it yourself. Nothing wears away trust as quickly as someone who does not practice what he preaches.

5. *Admit your mistakes.*

It is going to happen. You will do something thoughtless or reckless that hurts someone who has trusted you and been there for you. The worst thing you can do is to take someone on your support team for granted and assume that they will give you the benefit of the doubt. If you screw up, if you hurt someone through thoughtless action, go to the person you have wronged and make it right. Otherwise, don't expect the relationship to continue. **189**

▪ How Supportive Are You?

Building your dream team is a two-way street; you need to be there to support and encourage your friends as well as expect support from them. The best team situations occur when everyone plays a role and teammates are mutually supportive of each other.

Based on the five tips for growing your support team, see how supportive you are by answering the following questions.

Think of two or three key relationships you have with people—the relationships that you feel are most supportive and helpful to you. Are these relationships mutually beneficial, or are they slanted toward your needs only?

_____

_____

How do you feel when someone leans on you for support and you are able to come through and meet the needs of that person?

_____

_____

Are you able to pick up on issues in your friends' lives, issues that they may need support on? Do you pay attention to the details in your friends' lives?

_____

_____

Are you able to keep your word to someone, even if it means you have to sacrifice something? Can you recall a time when you did keep your word, even when it was hard for you to do so?

_____

_____

How did you feel in that situation? Were you glad you were able to keep your word, or did you resent that you had to do it?

_____

_____

How do you think your friend felt about you keeping your word, even though it meant you had to sacrifice something?

_____

_____

Do you expect more from your friends than you expect from yourself?

_____

_____

TEENS CAN MAKE IT HAPPEN

If you do expect more from your friends than from yourself, how do you think this makes your friends feel?

_____

_____

Think of a time when you made a mistake that hurt a relationship, and you didn't admit your mistake. What was the result with the relationship?

_____

_____

Now think of a time when you made a hurtful mistake, but you were big enough to admit it. How did your admission affect the relationship?

_____

_____

The good news you learned from this chapter is that you don't have to go it alone in the Success Process. In fact, you really *can't* go it alone and be very successful. Instead you need to cultivate good, trusting relationships with a variety of people who can support you as you work toward your goals. And you have to be supportive of those who need you, too. Achievements are greater and more lasting when accomplished through a team effort, be it a formal team, as in sports or clubs, or an informal team, such as through family, friends, and mentors.

Next we'll look at another crucial area in the Success Process: the ability to make good decisions. The difference between success and setback often lies in the decisions made along the way.

9 Win by a Decision

Think like a man of action. Act like a man of thought.

Henri Bergson

Robert Earl Love was a tall and skinny child, and always so *hungry* that his friends called him "Butterbean." He grew up with a very bad stutter that frustrated him, but Butterbean was able to release his frustrations on the basketball court. His basketball skills earned him a scholarship at tiny Southern University, and he eventually made it into the National Basketball Association, where he bounced around for several years as a backup player until the Chicago Bulls got him in 1968 as part of a trade for a player thought to be much better.

For seven straight seasons, Bob "Butterbean" Love led the Bulls in scoring while also earning a reputation as one of the toughest defensive players in the league. While he had long dreamed of proving himself through his basketball, Love later said that his real dream all those years was that he would start to speak "and the words would just flow out of my mouth."

When his athletic career ended, Butterbean could not find meaningful work because of his speech impediment. A proud man, he was forced to take work as a busboy and dishwasher, where, instead of feeling demeaned, he endeavored to be "the best dishwasher and busboy" he could be. His bosses praised his hard work but told him that he would never be promoted because of his inability to speak. Butterbean might have spent the rest of his life in that lowly work, but at the age of forty-five, he made a decision to pursue a better life.

Butterbean went to a speech therapist and applied the hard work and dedication to pursuing a vision for himself. Many people who knew him doubted that Bob Love could ever overcome his speech impediment, particularly when he had gotten such a late start at speech therapy. But he did it. He is now a goodwill ambassador for the Chicago Bulls, traveling around the city and the country speaking to adults and children in large groups. He does it joyfully, and although he still has to work to overcome his impediment, most of the time the words really do flow out of his mouth.

Bob Love is an example of what you can do when you make a decision to pursue a fulfilling life even when it appears that there is nothing you can do, even when you have had failures in the past. The ability to make decisions to better your life is crucial to the Success Process. If you can't make decisions and take action, you won't break free and create opportunities where none appeared to exist.

You may not have a speech impediment to overcome, but you will face decisions today, tomorrow, and throughout your life, many of which can alter your life for better or worse. Your ability to make good decisions will directly affect your life. In this chapter you'll learn how to

- Shape your life through your decisions,
- Recognize good and bad decisions,
- Realize when you are procrastinating and learn how to stop it,
- Make good decisions a habit,
- Use both your mind and your heart—logic and emotion—in making good decisions, and
- Follow a process that will help you make good decisions throughout your life.

We'll begin with the big picture first: shaping your life through decisions.

Shaping Your Life through Your Decisions

Even if you master all of the steps that we have covered so far in this book, you will fall short in your efforts to seek a rewarding life if you have difficulty making decisions. You might have goals and a vision for where you want to go; you might have a plan, and you might possess the courage to take risks and make changes. But if you don't have a method for making good decisions, you'll find yourself stumbling over and over again.

Some people are afraid to make decisions because they are afraid to move from what is known into the unknown. Some fear the decision-making process because it exposes them to criticism and evaluation. They don't want to

be wrong, ever. Decision making is such an important skill, yet we receive little training in how to go about it.

What you are in this world is largely the result of the decisions you make. That's right, *your* decisions. No one else can make the important decisions for you, and no one else *should* make them for you. You are not the victim of circumstances that happen *to* you; you are the maker of decisions that can work *for* you. You are free to make your decisions. You have that right. You have the power to choose by making decisions. If you are not happy with where you are in life, or if you think you can do better, then you can decide to do something different.

> The best thing that happened to me was getting busted for drugs. Before then, I didn't see any other road for me. That was just what was going on. But getting busted was my wake-up call. I figured I better choose another route quick because I didn't like where this one was going.
>
> Louie, age 19

We all have the ability to change our lives at any time—whether that means going from something bad to something good, or from something good to something even better. One of the best decisions I ever made was to leave one of the best jobs I've ever had. Life is about making choices, choosing paths, and all of our lives we struggle with making the right decisions. I see life as a series of paths taken and paths not taken. If you don't develop a consistent method for choosing yours, you will surely waste precious time and effort.

As director of education at the federal prison in Chicago, I was in a position to make a tremendous impact on the lives of men who had made many poor choices in the past. It was a challenging, tough, and constantly stimulating job. Believe me, federal prison inmates do not give you any opportunity to coast. They are always challenging you, prodding for signs of weakness or for an opening to somehow get one up on you.

It was like a chess game with far more serious consequences. There were many aspects of that job that I enjoyed, and the opportunity for advancement was good, but other opportunities were opening up for me, too. I had met Bob Brown through mutual friends, and he introduced me to his vast network in public relations and marketing. As a former assistant to the president of the United States, Bob was wired into the highest levels of business and politics. I knew that working with him would expand my horizons, and even though I was giving up a great deal of job security, I made the decision to make a career switch.

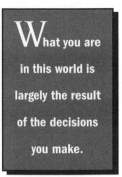

What you are in this world is largely the result of the decisions you make.

It opened up an entire new world of opportunity for me. It put me in a position to pair my lifelong interest in sports with my growing interest in business. At the time, though, it was a difficult decision to make. I had not yet learned to master the decision-making process that I am going to teach you in this chapter. I made a good decision, but sometimes knowing whether a decision is good or bad isn't easy to tell up front.

Recognizing Good and Bad Decisions

How do you know if you are making good decisions in your life? Here are some characteristics of good decisions. Good decisions

- open opportunities;
- make you feel good about yourself;
- allow you to express your talents, skills, and knowledge;
- silence your critics;
- move you closer to your goals;
- cause you to always look to the future;
- reduce your frustrations and anger;
- increase your potential; and
- attract dynamic people to your cause.

How do you know if you are making bad decisions? Here are some characteristics of bad decisions. Bad decisions

- put you on a dead-end street;
- result in second thoughts;
- cause you to look over your shoulder;

- inspire feelings of regret;
- are a lure for critics;
- bring trouble to your life; and
- attract predators who hope to capitalize on more bad decisions.

Obviously, if you want to pursue a fulfilling life, you need a process for making good decisions. Big decisions require big thinking and good information. Often, the only difference between you and someone you admire is that they have made the decision to make their lives better. There is a traditional African proverb that says, "If it is to be, it's up to me." Judith Jamison was writing about taking responsibility for decisions when she wrote, "The stars are in the sky. And I'm a person. I have a God-given talent, but I'm still that person, just like you, with two arms and two legs, and I decided to take it someplace."

Napoleon Hill, author of the classic *Think and Grow Rich,* has noted that successful people make decisions quickly and firmly once they have reviewed all of the information available. Unsuccessful people, he said, make decisions slowly and change them often. He claimed also that ninety-eight out of a hundred people never make up their minds about their major purpose in life because *they simply can't make a decision and stick with it.* I hope to help you become one of those people who can make good life decisions.

■ Decisions, Decisions, Decisions

We all make decisions every day. Unfortunately, most of us fail to recognize how important it is that we do our best to make good decisions. To make good decisions, you need to assess your personal strengths, needs, and resources, then check them against your Rules of the Road.

Write an example of a good decision you have made for yourself.

_____

_____

Now refer to the list of characteristics for good and bad decisions. Which characteristics of good decisions does it reflect?

_____

_____

_____

_____

Now write an example of a bad decision you have made for yourself.

_____

_____

Which characteristics of bad decisions does it reflect?

_____

_____

_____

_____

It's always easy to second-guess yourself. To be successful in life, you need to be able to think about the consequences of your decisions before you make them. Write down a decision you need to make, then use the list of characteristics of good and bad decisions to help you decide what to do. Remember this: It's often harder to make the best decision, but the long-term results of good decisions will always outweigh the short-term benefits of bad ones.

I need to decide . . .

_____

_____

Based on the characteristics of good and bad decisions, my decision is to . . .

_____

_____

I am deciding to do that because it reflects these characteristics of good decisions:

_____

_____

_____

_____

Putting Off Procrastination

One of the biggest obstacles to the decision-making process is something I am very familiar with: procrastination. I've worked at overcoming my tendency to procrastinate, which is the tendency to put things off. I come from a

long line of procrastinators. It might be longer, but they kept putting off having more of us. Mark Twain was the literary hero of procrastinators. His motto was *Never put off till tomorrow what you can do the day after tomorrow.*

Not making a decision is a decision in itself, one with many implications. One in five Americans is a chronic procrastinator, according to DePaul University professor Joseph R. Ferrari, coauthor of *Procrastination and Task Avoidance: Theory, Research and Treatment.*

Ferrari has identified two types of procrastinators: the *arousal* type and the *avoidance* type. The first type puts things off because they get a thrill out of doing things in a last-minute rush and at the buzzer. If you put off writing papers and doing assignments until the last moment, you know a little something about this type of procrastination. The second type puts things off to avoid them for various reasons, ranging from fear of failure to wanting to avoid unpleasant things. Those who procrastinate because they have a fear of failure believe that they are better off not trying than trying and failing. They don't realize that not to try is the biggest failure of all.

Understanding Procrastinators

Procrastinators come in all shapes and sizes, but here are a few common phrases you'll hear from serious procrastinators:

- This isn't the right time to make that decision.
- I have a few other things to deal with first.
- I don't have time for that.
- I've been meaning to get to that.
- I'll do that when I've got more experience.
- You wouldn't believe all the stuff I have to do before I can get to that.
- Tomorrow!
- I'm too distracted to do that.
- I'm waiting to make a bigger move.
- There is probably a safer (better, faster, easier) way of doing this. I'll wait for it.

Do any of those sound familiar to you? Procrastinators are creative in making excuses, even if they can't do anything else. The question they always get from people is "What are you waiting for?" Too often the unspoken answer is "The right time." "Right" meaning that everything is in place. Every variable is in your favor. For instance:

- You'll go out for basketball next year because so-and-so is graduating, your jump shot will be a little better, and you'll be a little stronger.
- You'll join in on a mentoring program for grade school students when you feel a little better about yourself, when you have a little more free time, and when your neighbor's child is old enough to be in the program and you can mentor her.
- You'll ask someone out when you lose about ten pounds, when your acne clears up, and when you can borrow your brother's car (which is never).

You get the picture. Perhaps you even recognize yourself *in* that picture. **199**
Decision-making gridlock is a serious problem if you are interested in pursuing your vision for a successful life. Often, it is based in fear, whether your particular brand is fear of success or fear of failure or just fear of pulling your head out of the ground, or wherever you might have stuck it. Think about the successful people you know. Are any of them procrastinators? Do they spend days looking before they leap? Or do they go after what they want? I was going to come up with eight tips to help you overcome this problem but I just don't have time right

now . . . just kidding. I'll get to those suggestions in a moment. First I want to explore a few theories behind procrastination.

The self-defeating habit of procrastination is a common trait. There are three theories as to why people put things off that are vitally important.

1. You are lazy.
2. You are self-destructive.
3. You like being stuck because it brings you sympathy.

As you can tell, these theories do not paint a pretty picture of the procrastinator's personality. None of them really explains the problem or deals with it in a very logical manner. No one is born lazy. Only truly demented people enjoy causing pain and mental torment to themselves. Sympathy may be one form of attention, but it is hardly uplifting or inspiring.

Recent studies of procrastination have found that people who put things off as a matter of habit are often troubled with feelings of hopelessness, low self-esteem, guilt, or fear. Procrastination is also the province of perfectionists, who put things off because they are waiting for the perfect time to produce the perfect results.

Regardless of the cause, you can take steps to get past procrastination.

Getting Past Procrastination

Here are eight tips to help my fellow procrastinators out there get beyond their "buts" and their "one day I'm gonnas."

1. *Take small bites.*

It's easy for procrastinators to put off large or complex projects or tasks, because they never have enough time to finish it all at once. Therefore, why start? Of course, with this attitude, you'll never finish the task, and it will loom larger and larger over your head until you get quite depressed or feel frantic about it.

Think in terms of one of those Mexican restaurants that advertises *Burritos As Big As Your Head.* They aren't exaggerating much. You don't order one and then say, "I think I'll wait for a better time to eat this." No, you get to work on it. You don't try to do it in one huge bite, however; you eat that giant burrito one small bite at a time. This is not only good for digestion; it is good for decision making.

2. *Begin now!*

Without giving yourself time to think of excuses, sit down now, start the process, and force yourself to keep at it for at least an hour. Set a time to pick up where you left off. This is a critical point, because one thing procrastinators aren't slow with is excuses. If you force yourself to do something *immediately,* you may surprise yourself at how pleased you are with the progress you make, and it may inspire you to keep at it a little at a time until you finish.

3. *Slam the door on critics.*

If you feel that you can't make a decision because someone is holding you back, break free of that sense of helplessness and victimization. Sometimes you have to go against the opinions of those around you in order to make the right decisions for yourself. You can't expect others to always share your vision. Don't let anything or anyone stand between you and your freedom to make decisions that improve your life. It is simply impossible to always reach a consensus.

4. *Lighten up.*

Procrastinators tend to take themselves far too seriously. The world is not focused on your every move. The stars will still shine tonight. The sun will still come up tomorrow. No matter what you do, the future of the galaxy is not resting on your shoulders. If the thought of making a decision is weighing so heavily that you can't make it, you need to step away and regain perspective so that you are not taking yourself so seriously. Do something to take your mind off of it and to lighten your mood. Take a walk, visit a friend who cheers you up, read a comic novel, or take in a comedy at the movie theater or on television. Get out of that dark mood.

5. *Think of the carrot, not the stick.*

Those who put things off sometimes do it because they focus on the difficulties and demands of taking an action rather than on the rewards that await them. How many times have you worried about doing something only to discover that it was not nearly as painful as you had imagined? Always keep in mind the rewards of taking action; don't focus so much on the problems of taking action that you are frozen in fear. When you make a decision that will be challenging for you to carry out but that will better your life, keep in mind how that action will ultimately reward you. If you lose that focus, you might lose your desire to act.

6. *Bring in a coach.*

These days people have personal fitness trainers, personal bankers, personal speech coaches, personal accountants, personal nutrition advisers. Why not bring in a friend or family member to be your anti-procrasti-

201

> With vision, you can choose to live in the moment, doing things with a purpose in mind, all leading toward making that vision happen.

nation coach? Give your coach a list of the things you need to do and order him or her to dog you until you do them. Provide the whip if you feel it is necessary. Chronic procrastination calls for drastic action.

7. *Live in the moment.*

I knew of a fellow who came to the end of his life and realized that he had accomplished nothing that he had wanted to do. He lamented this fact to a friend of his, saying "I don't know how I wasted my whole life." The friend observed that he hadn't started out to waste his whole life. First, he had wasted a minute of it, then an hour, then a day, then a week, a month, a year, a decade, and *then* his whole life. Take a clue and do the opposite. Use up every minute, every hour, every day, until you have made the most of your entire life. Be guided in your decisions by your vision for your life. When you have no vision, you have no real focus, and it's easy to waste time. With vision, you can choose to live in the moment, doing things with a purpose in mind, all leading toward making that vision happen.

8. *Don't demand perfection.*

Tell yourself there is not going to be a *perfect* time to get started, and that you don't have to be *perfect* in your performance. Compromise and start immediately; rough out the task and then build upon it. No one is standing over your shoulder demanding that you make no mistakes.

This is a problem I have. Because I spent so much of my life trying to prove my value and worth and to elevate my family's image, I became a perfectionist. It's funny, but trying to always be perfect often results in your not getting much of anything done. The pressure that perfectionists put on themselves is so intense because they can't possibly be perfect at all the things they set out to do. As a result, they get stuck. Believe me, I know. I am constantly telling myself to ease up, and to just take each task step by step, without fear that someone will criticize my work. This perfectionism was the main roadblock to making good decisions to better my life.

We often make things more difficult for ourselves by placing this sort of undue pressure on ourselves. Perfectionists get stuck because they feel they have to meet the standards of others, or their own unrealistic standards. They can never please themselves, because they feel they could have *always* done it better. Don't get caught in this trap. Make your expectations more realistic, and then focus not on your expectations, but on the work at hand.

■ "Mañana . . ."

"Mañana" is Spanish for "tomorrow," which is the procrastinator's favorite word. For procrastinators, tomorrow is the perfect time to start something; it's the procrastinator's battle cry.

Are *you* a procrastinator? If you put off doing this worksheet until tomorrow, we'll know you are . . . just kidding. Answer the following questions to check your "procrastination rating."

1. When faced with a large or complex task, you
   a. hide behind the couch until the task deadline has passed
   b. consider all the things you have to do to complete the task and get depressed
   c. make a game plan and then begin bit by bit
2. You have just been assigned to write a five-page paper for one of your classes. You react by
   a. going to a fast food restaurant because you an think better on a full stomach
   b. asking your friends what they are going to write about
   c. getting a start on your paper, even if it's to research what topic you want to write about
3. When you are in the middle of a project or task, and someone laughs and says, "Man, no way can *you* do that!" you
   a. agree with the person and say you must have had sunstroke when you took on the task
   b. say you could do it if you wanted, but you guess you didn't really want to do it right now
   c. tell the person to go take a hike, because this is important to you and you're going to do it
4. When a task appears to be larger than the world to you, you tell yourself
   a. that indeed it is monumental, the whole of humankind depends on you to accomplish this unattainable task, and thus all is gloom and misery, and there is no meaning to life anymore
   b. that you know it's really not that big; but it *feels* that big; and you're still stuck and gloomy
   c. that you're not performing brain surgery or curing cancer; the world— and you—will go on regardless of how you perform in this task
5. When faced with a difficult task, you tend to focus on
   a. the girl or boy you'd like to go out with

203

b. the difficulties involved, until they seem overwhelming

   c. the rewards at the end, which are tied directly to the purpose of doing the task in the first place

6. Because you have a history of procrastinating, you think it's a good idea for future tasks that you have some outside support and encouragement. Therefore you

   a. contact your local Procrastinators Anonymous organization, only to find out that their next meeting has been postponed

   b. enlist the support of your best friend, who is one of the founding members of your local Procrastinators Anonymous

   c. ask a friend or family member to hold you accountable and to help keep you on track

7. When you hear the phrase, "Seize the day!" you think of

   a. the battle cry of South American revolutionaries

   b. people who take on life with a zest, voraciously eating it up and looking for more, and you decide that fairly soon, when the time is right, you are going to be like that, too

   c. how you can make the most of every day, living with a purpose in mind and making decisions according to that purpose

8. You are faced with a difficult challenge and you find yourself in a familiar place: stuck. You realize your expectations for yourself are too high and are the reason you're stuck. You decide to

   a. give up and pretend you didn't care about the challenge in the first place

   b. wait until you have a little more time to tackle the challenge head on

   c. ease up on your expectations and not expect perfection, because you know you won't do anything otherwise

If you answered mainly *a*s or *b*s, you are a seasoned procrastinator and need to work on the eight points for getting past procrastination. If you answered mainly *c*s, you don't have problems with procrastination; you can make decisions and get to the task at hand. Congratulations!

Making Good Decisions a Habit

Before I introduce my decision-making process to you, I want to get you thinking about your own decision-making habits. You probably haven't given much thought to them because you make so many decisions in your life that the process becomes automatic.

Think for a moment about all of the decisions you have made in the last twenty-four hours. I'll bet you have decided, consciously or unconsciously, things such as:

- When to get out of bed,
- What to wear,
- What to have for breakfast,
- The way you're going to get to school,
- Where to sit in the school cafeteria,
- What to do after school,
- Which friends to call, and
- When to go to bed.

When you think about it, it is striking how many decisions you make every day, week, month, and year. But larger decisions aren't so automatic: You want to commit to a relationship but you've been burned before and are wary. You want to try out for a team or for a role in a play, but you don't want to embarrass yourself. You are considering taking a difficult class that you think will help you in the future, but you're not so sure you can do well in it.

Certainly you devote more time to larger decisions. Whether you go with grape jelly or strawberry, you will still have tasty toast. Green shirt or blue shirt, you'll still look good. But the choice of whether to take a challenging class or opt for an easier version—for instance, advanced calculus versus calculus—poses two very different options. If calculus is important to your education goals, and you feel advanced calculus will prepare you better for college, you may decide to take the advanced class, even though you might struggle some in it. If calculus is good background for your education goals, but taking the advanced class won't get you any closer to your long-term goals, then you will probably opt for the regular calculus class.

Making wise decisions is an integral part of life, and a major step in the Success Process. It's been said that we have no choice about our birth and none about death, but everything in between is ours to decide. The heart of the decision-making process lies in wisely choosing among the available alternatives. Is the reward equal to or greater than the risk? In other words, using the calculus example, is risking the struggle with the advanced class worth the rewards it will bring once you have completed it? Is going out for the school play worth the risk of not getting a part? The answers depend, of course, on your own goals and aspirations. These answers come from within. You can talk things over with friends and family, but the answers ultimately must come from *you.*

To make difficult decisions wisely, it helps to have a process for assessing each alternative and its consequences. Having a process will help you make decisions that are consistent with your values and principles, as well as your vision for a better life. It is also vital that you identify *as many alternatives as possible* when making a decision. You also need to be prepared to handle any criticism, which often accompanies a decision to make a change.

One advantage in making careful decisions is that people are apt to criticize you less when they know you've put a lot of thought into it before acting. Keep in mind that when you announce a decision to people for the first time, this is new information for them. They may be critical because they have not invested the same thought in it as you. They have not weighed the alternatives, as you have. Don't let their negative thinking affect you if you have carefully made this decision. The power of negative reactions and responses can cripple your ability to follow through on decisions.

The amount of time and effort you invest in making a particular decision depends how important and how difficult the decision is. Even with important decisions, however, many people too often follow the same casual process they use in daily decision making. They don't open their minds to all of the alternatives that may be available to them, and they don't think through all of the possible ramifications of each alternative.

For example, let's say Kevin, a high school senior, is deciding whether to go to college or enter the workforce straight out of high school. Kevin has worked a part-time job at minimum wage for two years. But he can get full-time work at more than double the minimum wage at a local factory or with a construction company.

Kevin is eager to be on his own. He likes the idea of earning his own money, being in his own apartment, and making what seems to be a lot of money. The alternative is to go through at least four more years of school, maybe working part-time jobs for a little spending money, and probably running up some debt through student loans that he'll have to start paying off once he graduates. He knows that the rewards might be greater later on, once he has a college degree, but he is anxious to get going *now*—not four years from now.

So he takes the factory or construction job, gets a small apartment, and laughs as his friends go to college and groan and complain about all the studying they have to do, and how they never have any money to do anything. But then they graduate, and with their degrees they get better-paying jobs than Kevin. In not too many years, they are making double what Kevin is making, and they are buying houses and cars while Kevin is still in his small apartment with the same car he's had since high school. He realizes he nibbled at the immediate reward of being on his own and earning money, as opposed to building on a greater vision and going through the steps to make that happen.

The good news, of course, is he can always decide to go back to school. He can always change. But many people fall into the trap of saying they're going to work for a few years and *then* go to college, and they never make it to college. They get stuck in their routine and never decide to change.

The moral of the story is simple: Consider all the ramifications of your decisions before you make them.

■ Learning from Your Past

Think back now and list three big decisions you have made in the last few years. They don't necessarily have to be *good* decisions—just three of the *biggest* decisions you have made.

Over the last few years my biggest decisions have included:

1. _____

2. _____

3. _____

What made these decisions *big?* The expense they involved? The amount of time they consumed? The changes they required you to make in your lifestyle or attitude? The risks involved?

Underneath each of those decisions, write down why it was so significant:

Decision 1. _____

    Significance _____

Decision 2. _____

    Significance _____

Decision 3. _____

    Significance _____

In looking back at these decisions and all that was involved, how do you feel now about the decisions you made? Did you make a good decision or a bad one? Note below whether each decision proved to be good or bad, and why.

Decision 1. _____

    It was good/bad because _____

Decision 2. _____

    It was good/bad because _____

Decision 3. _____

    It was good/bad because _____

Now think about *how* you made those big decisions, the process you used. Was it the same process you normally use in making your smaller daily decisions, or was it a more complex, thoughtful process? How did you arrive at your decision?

Decision 1. _____

    I decided to do this because _____

Decision 2. _____

    I decided to do this because _____

Decision 3. _____

    I decided to do this because _____

From your list, choose the most difficult decision you made. Beside it, list all of the alternatives you considered before making the decision:

The decision I faced was _____ .

The alternatives I considered included _____

_____ .

Now that some time has passed, were there any alternatives that you did not consider that, in retrospect, you should have included in the process of making the decision?

If so, what were they: _____

_____ .

Also, note what criticisms you were subjected to because of the decision you made. Below each one, write down the source of the criticism:

The criticism _____

    The critic _____

The criticism _____

    The critic _____

The criticism _____

    The critic _____

How did you handle this criticism? How did you respond to it?

_____

_____

Would your response be different today? If so, how?

_____

_____

Using Logic, Emotions, and a Positive Outlook

Some people like to make decisions based on pure logic, using only their minds. Others go more on feel, deciding based on their emotional response. Important matters require that you consider them with *both* your mind and your heart. Don't rely only on logic and put aside your emotions when it comes to making big decisions in your life.

Even after you have intellectually weighed a decision, there remains the matter of what you feel in your heart. Some call this your "gut instinct." It is an instinct based on past experiences and the emotional value you place on the decision.

209

I didn't even ask my parents about that party, because I just had this gut feeling that I shouldn't go. I knew there was going to be stuff going on there that I didn't want to get mixed up in. I was glad I didn't go—especially when I found out that police had raided the party and arrested a bunch of kids for underage drinking.

Terry, age 17

In *Emotional Intelligence,* Daniel Goleman notes that these gut instincts are emotional signals that alert us to the potential hazards of certain courses of action, but "they can also alert us to a golden opportunity." Most of the time, we don't immediately recall what past experience or recollection triggers the gut instinct reaction, but generally we follow that instinct based on the emotions it sets off. Goleman believes the key to sound personal decision making is to be tuned into your feelings. When you have a step-by-step decision-making process such as the one I am going to provide you with, it helps ensure that you intellectually *and* emotionally weigh *all* of the relevant information and the best available alternatives before making the decision.

There is one more aspect of decision making that you need to consider before I introduce you to my process. I am going to ask you to *smile* while you go through it. I know that may sound silly, but science is on my side on this one, too. Nearly fifty years after Dr. Norman Vincent Peale wrote *The Power of Positive Thinking,* behavioral scientists and others have come around to *his* way of thinking. Science once scoffed at the notion that positive thinking could seriously affect your physical and mental health, but not anymore. Research has shown that optimism not only is a helpful tool; it is one that can be *learned.* Negative thinking can cripple you mentally, spiritually, and physically, and it can also impede your ability to make decisions wisely. An optimistic and positive emotional approach to decision making, on the other hand, helps you to consider all the factors involved.

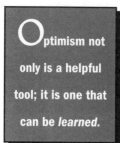

Optimism not only is a helpful tool; it is one that can be *learned.*

A positive approach opens your mind and makes you more flexible in your thinking and more capable of handling complex decisions. On the other hand, being in a foul mood can hamper your ability to make a good decision. Negative moods tend to promote fearful, biased, and overly cautious decision making. So before you make any important decision in your life, make sure that you are in the proper mood. Elevate your mood by going to a funny movie, reading a funny book, or socializing with upbeat people who make you laugh. Studies have shown that laughter prompts you to think more broadly and freely, which helps a great deal in making complex decisions with far-reaching impact.

The Winning-by-a-Decision Process

Now I'll present my process for making big decisions, using boxing as a metaphor for the process. The process is split into five steps:

1. The weigh-in,
2. Suiting up,
3. Checking the fit,
4. Stepping into the ring, and
5. Going for the knockout.

Step One: The Weigh-In

Big decisions often are spurred by your learning something that sheds new light or gives you a new perspective on an existing situation. This new information or perspective forces you to examine your situation and to *weigh* the possibilities for making a change.

You may have been perfectly happy with your old car until it broke down and a mechanic informs you that the new exhaust system for it will cost $500. Now you have to decide whether it's worth fixing and, if so, how you are going to pay for it. In a similar manner, I was fairly content in my job with the federal prison system until Bob Brown introduced me to the possibilities of a career in marketing and public relations. Suddenly, my vision for a better life expanded. I began to see how I could incorporate my love of sports with a career that still gave me the opportunity to work with people.

Now, sometimes the new information presented may force you to see that sticking with the old way or existing situation is even more risky than seeking change. The heavy smoker whose medical exam reveals serious lung damage will, hopefully, see the light and decide to change his or her behavior based on the new information.

The key questions to consider at this stage in the decision-making process are:

- Are the risks serious if I don't change?
- Do the benefits of changing outweigh the risks involved?

If the risks in your current behavior or situation aren't serious, then continuing on your current path is a workable option. Likewise, if the benefits of changing don't outweigh the risks involved in making the change, you might also consider staying on your current path. If, however, staying on your current path is risky, or if the benefits you would reap by making a change outweigh the risks involved in making the change, then you would be better off making the change.

Take the previous example of Kevin, the high school graduate who decides to go to work in the factory or with the construction company. What are the

risks that he faces with this decision? Job advancement might be relatively limited, as are potential earnings. Job boredom and dissatisfaction are high risks.
Certain factory and construction jobs involve physical risks. Taken together, these
risks appear to be pretty serious, though certainly many people who work factory
and construction jobs might refute this, because risk can be a highly personal and
subjective issue. However, most people would agree that these risks mentioned
are real risks.

Now let's look at the second question: Do the benefits of changing outweigh the risks involved? If Kevin goes to college, will he benefit more than if he
takes the construction or factory job? He risks doing poorly in college and flunk-
ing or dropping out, in which case he'd have been better off going directly into the
workforce. He also loses out on achieving his independence by immediately earning his own money. But in the long run, if he earns a degree, he is likely to benefit
by earning more money and, with it, greater job satisfaction. Again, this is a subjective call, but most people would say the benefits outweigh the risks involved.

Weighing the risks and benefits is not always easy. Variables are involved
that have no immediate answer attached. For instance, you don't know exactly
what type of job you may wind up with after college, especially if you're a liberal
arts major. But you can assume it will be more satisfying, challenging, and better
paying than most jobs you can obtain with only a high school education.

If the answer to the question *Are there serious risks involved if I don't
change?* is *Yes,* there are serious risks involved, then it is time to move to the next
step of the process.

Step Two: Suiting Up

The next step in the decision-making process is to identify as
many suitable alternative solutions or courses of action as possible. This is another step in the Success Process where it is useful to let your imagination run
wild, dreaming up as many possible solutions as you can, weighing them all, and
picking and choosing those that might appear to work.

Don't do this all on your own. Enlist members of your support team to
help you and seek expert advice if it is appropriate. For instance, Kevin, in making his decision about going to college or immediately going to work, could have
enlisted the help of his family, a few trusted teachers, his guidance counselor, and
others. He could have looked into a variety of colleges, including junior colleges.
It's in your best interest to seek as much information as you can about the issue.
Kevin made his choice on his own without considering much information at all.
What alternatives might he have seen if he had looked? Let's list a few. He could:

- Go to a four-year college or university and explore various areas of interest before deciding on a major.
- Enroll in a junior college and work part- or even full-time while attaining an associate's degree and leave his options open for a bachelor's degree.
- Enter a trade school to develop a trade and expand his possibilities for job satisfaction.
- Work as an apprentice for someone in a field he's truly interested in, with the idea that he might one day start his own business in that field.

The more information you have about an issue, the more you consider the issue from various perspectives as objectively as possible, the better you can decide what's best for you. Be open to all alternatives at this stage, even if some appear to be a bit wild. Sometimes we need to step outside of our boxes and consider things that appear to be unlikely solutions. Many times the greatest decisions are those that make you stray far from the beaten path. That's not necessarily bad, as this poem by Robert Frost attests:

The Road Not Taken

Two roads diverged in a yellow wood,
And sorry I could not travel both
And be one traveler, long I stood
And looked down one as far as I could
To where it bent in the undergrowth;
Then took the other, as just as fair,
And having perhaps the better claim,
Because it was grassy and wanted wear
Though as for that, the passing there
Had worn them really about the same,

And both that morning equally lay
In leaves no step had trodden black.
Oh, I kept the first for another day!
Yet knowing how way leads on to way,
I doubted if I should ever come back.

I shall be telling this with a sigh
Somewhere ages and ages hence:
Two roads diverged in a wood, and I—

213

I took the one less traveled by,
And that has made all the difference.

Step Three: Checking the Fit

> **M**any times the greatest decisions are those that make you stray far from the beaten path.

Once you have identified suitable alternatives, the next step is to mentally try each one on and check to see which best fits your vision for a better life. Carefully examine each alternative, get a feel for each, and evaluate the pros and cons of each. Examine them for both the short term and the long term and realize that short-term benefits might appear enticing, but they can come at the expense of greater long-term benefits. If you don't find any alternatives that match up with your vision for a better life, you may have to go back to Step Two and come up with more attractive alternatives.

The key questions at this stage are: *Which alternative is best?* and *Can the best alternative help me meet my goals?*

The appeal of the alternatives depends to a great degree upon your personal needs and goals. For instance, Kevin feels the need to be out on his own, fending for himself. He wants that freedom. He wants to be earning money now, dependent on no one, and answering to no one. He certainly would like to be satisfied in a job, but he figures deep down a job is a job; you put in your time and you get your money.

What Kevin may not realize is he will be dependent on someone and answering to someone—his boss. His livelihood depends on the market, but he doesn't realize that. He might do well to consider alternatives that include education and an eventual degree, because even though his livelihood will still be tied to the market, he will likely have greater flexibility and more marketable skills and greater degrees of responsibility.

Whatever the situation, at this stage of the decision-making process it is important to try on each alternative to decide which best suits you.

Step Four: Stepping into the Ring

At this point you are like an actor taking on a role. After identifying the alternative—or alternatives if you are torn between a number of choices—imagine yourself taking a particular course and consider the implications. What might happen if you take this route with your life? What will the effect be on your personal development and relationships, your future career, your place in the community? Will it move you along toward your vision for a better life?

Sometimes, of course, you may have to take a side road in your journey along the Success Process. Maybe Kevin's real dream is to own his own small company, be it in landscaping or woodworking or some business in which he combines his love of the outdoors with his desire to use his hands and get "down and dirty." If this is the case, he might be better off going to a trade school and combining that with an apprenticeship where he can really learn the trade. The immediate income would be lower, but the long-term payoff would be much higher and would help him toward his vision for himself. Again, regardless of the situation, when you walk into the ring mentally with each alternative, always keep your ultimate goal in mind.

As you try out the most appealing alternatives, you will develop a sense of which is the best choice for you and, without even realizing it, you will move closer to making a final decision. Now the key question becomes: *Should I make the decision?*

Step Five: Go for the Knockout!

Once you have committed to making a decision that you have carefully evaluated, you should be prepared to take it all the way without retreating. Know that there will be times when your decision will be challenged, but if you have followed each step in the process and given careful thought to your choices along the way, you should be able to face these challenges and overcome them.

What types of challenges might you face? Others may disapprove of your decision because of their own biases and self-interests. The risks that you foresaw will probably arise, and maybe also some that you had not anticipated. It could be that the scenario you envisioned will not unfold as you had thought it would. The benefits may not be as great or come as quickly. The downside may be worse than you imagined.

It is important to prepare yourself for such internal conflict and to always keep in mind your ultimate dreams of a successful life. Very little is accomplished without at least some sacrifice and temporary setbacks. You may have to go deep into your reserves of patience and resilience to manage the change. But always keep in mind that you made the decision carefully and thoughtfully and that ultimately it should move you closer to your dreams and goals.

■ The Decision Process

You've just read about the five steps to making good decisions:

- The weigh-in,
- Suiting up,
- Checking the fit,
- Stepping into the ring, and
- Going for the knockout.

Now take the time to work through a decision of your own, using this process.

■ Step One: The Weigh-In

Write down a decision that you are currently facing.

_____

_____

What are the risks you face if you don't decide to change your situation? Are they serious risks? Write them below:

_____

_____

What are the benefits of making the change?

_____

_____

Do they outweigh the risks? (Note: Choose an issue where you feel the benefits outweigh the risks—otherwise you have no need to go on to Step Two!)

_____

_____

■ Step Two: Suiting Up

Explore the alternatives that you can choose from in making the best decision. Be creative; think of as many solutions as you can.

1. _____

2. _____

3. _____

4. _____

5. _____

■ Step Three: Checking the Fit

An effective way to check the fit of each alternative is to create a *Decision Balance Sheet*. In the space below, write down one alternative that appears to be strong.

Alternative #1 _____

_____

_____

Now, list the pros and cons of this alternative in each category listed:

Your Personal Development

Pros	Cons
_____	_____
_____	_____
_____	_____
_____	_____

Your Career

Pros	Cons
_____	_____
_____	_____
_____	_____
_____	_____

Your Relationships

Pros	Cons
_____	_____
_____	_____
_____	_____
_____	_____

Now review the pros and cons in each area of your life. When you find one on each side that appears to balance each other out, cross them out. If you find one pro that seems to equal to two cons, cross all three out. If you find two cons equal to three pros, cross out all five. Do this with every possible alternative until you determine whether its impact on your life would be positive or negative overall. This is a subjective way of measuring a decision's appeal to you; if nothing else it makes you thoroughly think through each alternative.

Note that there are two types of errors that you may be likely to make in completing the balance sheet:

1. You may overlook cons because you are reluctant to admit the potential for negative results.
2. You may be overly optimistic in projecting pros.

Remember that this has to be a thoroughly honest process; otherwise it is invalid. By being candid and thoughtful at this stage, you can save yourself a great deal of regret down the road.

▪ Step Four: Stepping into the Ring

Now imagine that you have identified the best alternative after weighing the pros and cons, and answer these questions:

What impact will it have on your personal development?

_____

_____

On your career?

_____

_____

On your relationships?

_____

_____

How will it move you toward your vision for a better life?

_____

_____

Making decisions can be a difficult process. Mastering the process is essential to your ability to shape your life and move toward your vision. And the decision-making process is one that is closely connected to the topic in the final chapter: that of committing to your vision. Decisions and commitments are intertwined. Good decisions can help you stay committed to your vision even in the face of adversity.

10 Commit to Your Vision

Remember to always dream. More importantly, to make those dreams come true and never give up.

Dr. Robert D. Ballard

You've come a long way in learning the Success Process. Through the first eight steps, you've learned how to

- be more self-aware and know what your gifts and talents are,
- create your vision for your life,
- develop plans that will help make your vision happen,

- employ some Rules of the Road to keep you on track,
- take the risks necessary to move forward,
- adapt to change and make change work *for* you rather than *against* you,
- use teamwork and the support of others to adapt to changes and to reach your goals, and
- shape your life through wise decisions.

The final piece to the puzzle is commitment to your vision. You surely will be tested along the way, and without commitment you won't be able to overcome the challenges and obstacles that you will face. Let me tell you a brief story to show you the power of commitment.

Before I became director of education at the federal prison in Chicago, which was a job that I enjoyed, I briefly had one of the worst jobs of my life. I transferred to Chicago from the federal prison near Denver, where I had been in an administrative job, but the only position available at the time in the Chicago facility was in Receiving and Discharge. I already had a master's degree in education, but I wasn't putting it to much use in this job. My duty was to help process and search inmates coming into and going from the prison. Obviously they weren't very happy to be there, and neither was I.

I hated that job with a passion, but I never let anyone know it. It may well have been one of the worst jobs in the building, but I had the best attitude of any employee there. My coworkers and supervisors would ask how it was going and I would tell them "Great, just great." I was determined not to complain. Instead, I committed myself to being such a positive and dedicated employee that my supervisors would have no choice but to promote me.

My plan was to show that I could stand out even in a bad position. Since the rewards of the job were nonexistent, I sought other opportunities to show my leadership abilities. I became president of the employees' club and worked in my off hours to make conditions better for my coworkers. I contributed to the employee newsletter. I did everything I could to rise above my circumstances and to focus instead on the possibilities.

It worked. One day the warden came by and asked how I was doing in my job, and I told him I was doing the best I could to make everything run smoothly for him. Within a very short time, I was asked to apply for the job of supervisor of education at the prison. My boss told me that I had impressed everyone with my positive attitude toward a job that they knew I must have found unchallenging. I changed my circumstances by committing myself to rise above a bad situation. My goal was to do that bad job so well that my supervisors would have to promote me, and they did.

There is great power in making a commitment to bettering your life. When you dedicate yourself to rising above your circumstances, you will rise.

221

When you let the people around you know that you not only *want* something better, but you are *dedicated* to it, they buy into your vision of yourself. They become your cheerleaders and champions.

Why is it that we cheer the underdogs in sporting events and movies? Why do the benchwarmers who play with enthusiasm draw cheers as great as the stars when they enter a game? Because the fans sense a *commitment* to the game in those players, too. They want to reward that commitment. That is part of the human spirit. We want to see those who strive succeed.

That success often only comes with firm commitment. In this chapter you'll learn how to

- commit to bettering your life,
- create positive energy from your commitments,
- honor your commitments,
- pursue your vision with enthusiasm, and
- make commitments part of your everyday life.

Committing to Better Your Life

Committing to better your life means never giving up, never giving in, never losing your focus and your desire to better yourself, whether in your relationships or personal development, your education or career, or your role as a positive force in your community.

Each of the steps I have provided you with is vital, and the final one is as important as any. If you don't fully commit yourself to better your life, how will you ever rise above difficult circumstances and obstacles in your path?

All the other steps directly affect your commitment. Consider:

- Knowing who you are and what your talents and gifts are will help you stay committed to better your life and use those talents and gifts.
- Your vision and your plan act as anchors when the winds of trouble want to blow you away.

- Having your Rules of the Road in place helps you to find and keep your way.
- Taking risks to move forward and adapting to change would be awfully hard to do without a firm commitment to your vision.
- A support team can offer encouragement and advice and help you stay committed.

All the steps work together to make your vision happen.

What does it mean to make a commitment? It means persevering and holding on to your dreams and goals no matter how difficult the circumstances. It means valuing and believing in your vision more than you fear the dangers and obstacles that await you It means focusing on your vision and taking necessary risks because you are worth it, and you deserve a fulfilling life.

> When you have a vision and a solid plan in mind, and you are committed to that vision and plan, nothing can stop you. When people fail to fulfill their vision, it is almost always because they stop themselves. They see a high wall that they have to scale, and they say, "Surely I can't scale that wall. No one could expect me to do that." And so they sink back into their present circumstances.

When you are committed to your vision, you have to *expect* good things to happen—no matter what the odds, no matter what logic whispers in your ear, no matter what other people might tell you. Had David listened to logic and to the people around him, he would never have had the courage or the boldness to challenge Goliath. No one expected David to be victorious; all the counsel was to avoid confrontation. But David had a very different vision, and a total commitment to that vision. He acted on that vision and he accomplished the unbelievable.

David was just a young man, flesh and blood just like you. Things are no different for you. You have a choice, just as David did. You can live in fear and shrink back at challenges, like the other Israelites, or you can step up, fully committed to your vision, like David.

Let me give you two modern-day examples of commitment.

Overcoming Great Odds

Two Olympians from the 1988 Olympics in Calgary stood out, not so much for how they performed, but for how committed they were to their dreams of athletic achieve-

> When you have a vision and a solid plan in mind, and you are committed to that vision and plan, nothing can stop you.

ment. One of them was Dan Jansen, the young man from West Allis, Wisconsin, who had been the favorite to win the gold in both the 500- and 1,000-meter speed skating events. Just seven hours before his first race started, however, Dan's sister Jane died of leukemia. Her death had not been unexpected, but it was still devastating for Dan, who had been extremely close to her. He decided to skate and to dedicate his performance to her memory, but when he stepped up to the starting line for the 500-meter race, he appeared to be dazed.

The emotional anguish in his expression and the obvious inner battle between his feelings for his sister and his desire to compete made for a powerful moment. People around the world were moved by the courage he showed in even attempting to race.

Distracted by the tragedy of his sister's death, he tripped and fell shortly into the race. His powerful body simply could not carry the weight of his shattered emotions. Then, three nights later, the world was pulling for him again as he got off to a winning pace in the 1,000-meter event. But again the inner turmoil took its toll. With the world watching, this great athlete fell again. Dan Jansen failed, but he was not defeated. He was still committed to his dream. "I'll be back," he promised his supporters.

Olympic officials rewarded Jansen's courage and his obvious commitment to his sport by giving him the Olympic Spirit Award that year. After having difficulty and performing poorly in the 1992 Olympics, Jansen honored his commitment by staying in competition for the 1994 Olympics. There, although he very nearly fell again, Dan set a world record and took the gold in the 1,000-meter race. Jansen's commitment to his sport and to his own athletic ability is inspiring and moving. The world's reaction to his struggle and his ultimate achievement of his vision for Olympic gold says a great deal to me about our high regard for commitment, and so does the response to another courageous athlete at Calgary whose performance prompted as much laughter as Jansen's provoked tears.

Soaring Like an Eagle

Unlike the powerfully built Jansen, this athlete was a strange bird who wanted to fly, and believe me, even though he could barely get off the ground, his spirit soared. Blind in one eye, with the athletic grace of an albatross in a headwind, Eddie "the Eagle" Edwards, a plasterer by trade, was the first British ski jumper in Olympic history, which was not surprising, since England has no ski jumps. Eddie was twenty-four years old and had only been ski jumping two years when he committed to his vision of competing in the Olympic games.

He had no coach, no financial support, no equipment. So he chopped wood, washed dishes, swept floors, and ate table scraps to save money so that he could train in Finland for the 1988 Olympics. Still, he had so little money that he lived in a mental hospital there because the rate was only two dollars a night.

In truth, Eddie the Eagle was not an Olympic-caliber ski jumper. But he had heart and commitment to a dream, and every time he stood at the top of the jump, people all over the world cheered that he would surpass his own dreams and win an Olympic medal. Eddie did have his best jump ever in the 90-meter competition. It was 155 feet, ten inches short of the winning jump, but the crowd cheered as though Eddie the Eagle had set a world record.

Why did so many people cheer this poor, nearsighted plasterer? Eddie knew. "People had read about the struggle I had to make the Olympics, which was my dream, and they could see that dreams come true," he said afterward. When we cheer for underdogs such as Eddie the Eagle, we are applauding their drive, their positive energy, their vision, and, most of all, their commitment to their dreams and goals.

Living Out Your Commitment

I told you earlier of my assistant, Chris, who wanted to break into sports marketing so badly that he offered to work for free. In sharing his commitment with me, Chris created positive energy that charged me up and made me accept his vision of himself. I plugged into Chris's dream because of that positive energy. Out of nothing—no experience, no job opening—he changed his circumstances. He bettered his life with nothing more than his commitment.

How could Chris take such a risk? How could Dan Jansen ever have found the strength to continue his athletic career through three Olympics unless he was totally committed to his dream of winning a gold medal? How could Eddie the Eagle have found the courage to fly if it were not for his great commitment to simply compete in the Olympics?

A commitment is not some vague promise to yourself that you will do something. A commitment is something you *live*. Everything you do is a reflection of your commitment. Every approach you take to your life, the good times and the hard times, is an expression of that commitment.

A true commitment is the focusing of energy toward a purpose or cause. It is *doing* rather than *saying*. It is persevering and continuing to pursue your vision in spite of distractions, hardships, criticism, and risk. It is doing something because you believe it is right for you to do it. Why is this so important? Because the commitments you choose to make and to fulfill in your life ultimately shape your life.

You can make a lot of mistakes on the journey to a fulfilling life without seriously harming your ability to achieve your dream. But it will not happen if you

225

make the mistake of failing to commit yourself fully to your vision. No one can help you overcome a lack of commitment to your own life. If you don't have it, no one can provide it for you. You must demand it of yourself.

And when you do demand it of yourself, be ready for great things to happen:

- You can overcome an impoverished life.
- You can stay or get free from tobacco, alcohol, and other drugs, as well as other self-defeating behaviors.
- You can rise above any hopelessness and despair that surrounds you.
- You can transform low self-esteem into healthy self-esteem and make your vision grow from small to big, from ordinary to extraordinary.
- You can turn away from the things that are damaging and defeating in your life and turn toward the things that are positive and healthy and good.
- You can turn from doubt and pessimism to confidence and optimism.
- You can achieve your goals by following a wise plan and staying committed.
- You can lift yourself out of any muck and mire that you're in, beginning today. Beginning right now.

> A true commitment is *doing* rather than *saying*. It is persevering and continuing to pursue your vision in spite of distractions, hardships, criticism, and risk.

You can do amazing things when you are committed to doing them. Notice I don't say you can achieve whatever you want easily. You need to be committed for the very reason that achievement *won't* come easily. But if you want it, and you have a wise plan in place, and you follow the plan and take risks and adapt to change and lean on others when you need to, you can make it. You can do it if you're committed to doing it.

■ Keeping Commitments

Write down some commitments you have made already in your life, such as your commitment to your family, to your friends, to a relationship, to sports or other pursuits, to a social cause, or to a career path.

I have committed to: _____

_____

_____

_____

Next, for each commitment that you have *kept,* note the positive results in your life.

Commitment kept _____

    Result _____

Commitment kept _____

    Result _____

Commitment kept _____

    Result _____

Now note some commitments that you have not been able to keep.

_____

_____

_____

_____

Note why you were not able to keep these commitments. Be honest with yourself; you can only learn from your past when you're honest about it.

_____

_____

_____

_____

What was the result of not being able to keep these commitments?

_____

_____

_____

_____

Write down some small commitments that you can make in the coming days and weeks in order to build your power to keep commitments. For example, commit to reading an inspiring book about someone such as Nelson Mandela, who committed his life to freeing his nation from apartheid; or Martin Luther King Jr., who fought for civil rights and changed this nation just as Mandela changed his.

In the next week, I commit to three actions that will move me closer to my vision of a better life:

1. _____

2. _____

3. _____

Creating Positive Energy from Your Commitments

The commitments in your life obviously have a great impact on the quality of life you lead. Being committed to goals and principles and to living a better life creates positive energy that affects all areas of your life. Other than my commitment to myself, I had absolutely no reason to dig in and give my best effort to that terrible job in Receiving and Discharge. No reason other than a commitment to creating positive energy that would propel me right out of that job. What if I had decided that the job was not worth my effort? What if I had gone to my supervisors and said, "This job is beneath me"? Would that have made me a more valuable employee in their eyes?

I made a commitment when I took that job to do it to the best of my abilities. If I had failed to honor that commitment, I would have dishonored myself. I believe that anytime you fail or abandon a commitment, you lose a little of yourself.

> I got into this situation in this summer job where a friend and I could slack off because we weren't very closely supervised. We could sort of make it look like we were doing more than we actually did, or we could use other people as excuses. We thought it was pretty cool. But I got bored stiff, and by the end of the summer I thought, "What a waste of time. I didn't learn a thing, and I didn't get anything out of it." And I realized I didn't get anything out of it because, well, I didn't put anything into it.
>
> Jim, age 18

You can't fake commitment. You either put everything into it or you don't. Have you ever witnessed someone competing in a game who wasn't really committed to winning? It wasn't hard to pick that person out, was it? That person may have *thought* he was committed to playing, but his actions told the truth.

Commitment is giving all that you have to get all that you want. So many people who are unhappy with their lives or circumstances miss this point. They seem to think the answer is to complain, but what good does it do to attack a negative situation with negative attitudes and behavior? That approach reflects a *victim's mentality.* They blame. They foster resentment and anger. And they just don't get it.

Nobody cheers for a player with a bad attitude. Bosses don't look to promote the worker who complains or does a tough job poorly. The world in general does not respond to negative energy. Think back to the unfulfilled commitments you listed on your worksheet. What sort of positive energy came out of those unfulfilled commitments? Do I need to even provide a line for your response? I don't think so.

Commitment is giving all that you have to get all that you want.

Making a commitment is like exercising a muscle. It has to be worked and tested and strengthened over time. If you make small commitments such as doing your class assignments, showing up for baseball or band practice, eating right and getting regular exercise, and then don't keep them, how will you honor your greater commitments to yourself and others?

Commitment is the capacity for setting goals and achieving them. That capacity can be enlarged only through exercising your power to make commitments and fulfilling them. When you do, you will create a positive energy that will help you continue to keep your commitments. You will begin to realize that you *can* do what you set out to do. This will propel you to greater and greater achievements.

Honoring Your Commitments

Keeping a commitment is a major step forward, but breaking one is a step back. Don't make commitments that you can't keep; otherwise, you will never advance toward your vision of a rewarding life. Make commitments wisely and only after careful consideration. If you overload yourself with responsibilities, you will succeed only in frustrating yourself and those around you.

When you keep commitments, you build your confidence and begin to break free from circumstances that have held you back. Stephen Covey teaches that the first step in getting unstuck with your life is to *stop breaking commitments to yourself.* If you tell yourself you are going to do something, you have to do it; otherwise you'll never be free to pursue your vision for your life. Imagine volunteering to coach a Little League team and then failing to show up. How many lives are affected when that commitment is not fulfilled?

When you keep your commitments, you build trust in yourself and with others. Commitments are promises, and each commitment that you make and stick with is a goal achieved. Each goal that you achieve is another indication that you are guided by the possibilities of your life rather than the circumstances.

Too many people give only lip service to "making a commitment." They mentally embrace the idea without performing the action. Making a commitment means devoting your time and effort to achieving objectives. Commitments can be very broad and involve virtually all aspects of your life, such as a commitment to live a more healthy life. They can also be very specific, such as a commitment to earn all As and Bs this semester, or to earn an A in a particular class. Each commitment, however, is directed toward achieving specific *results,* regardless of whether a commitment is general or specific.

For example, here are some general commitments:

- I'm going to start eating better.
- I'm going to start working out regularly.
- I'm going to put more time into my studies.
- I'm going to learn how to play piano.

Now here are some specific commitments, playing off those four general commitments:

- I'm going to cut out the french fries when I eat fast food.
- I'm going to start jogging four times a week and lifting weights twice a week.
- I'm going to study from 4 P.M to 6 P.M. every weeknight.
- I'm going to take piano lessons once a week and practice one hour a day.

Regardless of the type of commitment you make, you have to put some real energy into it.

Pursuing Your Vision with Enthusiasm

To be committed, you have to have goals, and you have to have vision and *enthusiasm* about avidly pursuing that vision. Emerson said, "Nothing great is ever achieved without enthusiasm."

Enthusiasm comes with an emotional commitment to a vision, goal, or dream. It comes when you pursue your goals as if your life depends on it (and believe me, it does!). Understand that your life depends not on your goals, but on your *pursuit* of those goals, because when you are leading a life with direction and purpose and enthusiasm, you are truly *living*.

Think about the people you know who seem to be just going through the motions. What do they have in common? They lack direction. They have no enthusiasm. The thought of a challenge sends them fleeing in terror back to their La-Z-Boy recliners, back to the television, back to the street-corner hangout, back to a life going nowhere fast.

Now, think about the people you know who are full of life. What do they all share? A purpose and direction. An enthusiasm for life. A joy in what they are doing. A willingness to face challenges and overcome them. Being mentally and emotionally committed to *enthusiastically* pursuing your vision for a better life is vital for five reasons.

1. *You can meet challenges.*

You can respond in one of two ways when your vision for a better life is challenged. You can give up or step up. If you are enthusiastic and committed to bettering your life, you'll step up and accept challenges as opportunities for growth. If you are uncommitted, you'll retreat. Enthusiasm helps you overcome obstacles in your path along the Success Process. Remember, this process is a long-distance run, not a short sprint. You can't expect to achieve your dreams with a short burst of speed. Only a deep emotional commitment and the enthusiasm and energy that come with it will get you through the long haul.

I used to stay far away from challenges. I was afraid that people would see that I couldn't do everything I wanted to do. But I found myself forced into a couple of challenges and really learned from them. I realized you have to take the challenges if you want to do whatever it is you set out to do.

Tina, age 17

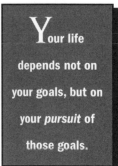

Your life depends not on your goals, but on your *pursuit* of those goals.

2. *You can develop your talents.*

When you are committed and enthusiastic, you make it possible for all of your talents to be developed and put to their highest use. Why do so many people go to their graves with their talents and gifts untapped? Think about that next time you walk past a cemetery. How might the world be different had everyone gone to their graves only after their talents have been allowed to fully blossom? That is accomplished only by commitment and enthusiasm, by constantly striving to tap into the deepest reserves, pulling out all that is within you and unleashing those gifts granted you.

I look at it this way: If you don't use your talents, what's the use of having them? It's like having a million dollars but never spending any of it or investing it. You just let it sit. What's the point in that?

Lisa, age 16

3. *You can rev up for risks.*

Imagine yourself on a bridge over a river. As you cross the bridge, you look down and see a key on a log floating by. It's just a worn key, nothing special, so you pay it no mind and continue on your way. It doesn't enter your mind to dive into the water and retrieve that key.

Now, look again. Instead of a worn key, you realize that the key will unlock the door to an opportunity that is really important to you. It's the key to getting into the college of your choice, entering and prospering in the career of your choice, developing and using your most cherished gifts. In short, it's the key to living a satisfying and fulfilling life. For that, you not only are willing to consider taking a risk, you are *enthusiastic* about taking that risk. You find yourself leaping over the railing and swimming after the key on that log because you have a vision of what that key can do for your life. You have become emotionally and enthusiastically *committed* to the goal of retrieving that key before it floats out of sight.

Emotional commitment and enthusiasm will have that effect on you. It will rev you up to take the risks that you need to take. Without them, you can't see the value of taking risks, and therefore you are not willing to make the leap. If you don't have your heart into your pursuit of a satisfying life, you won't be willing to take the risks that are essential.

I decided to take up wrestling for the first time as a junior. We have a real strong program at our school—we finished fourth in state last year. My coach said,

"There are plenty of guys ahead of you, and you don't have any experience." I told him that was okay; I was ready to go. He said, "Our practices are hard. You'll sweat more than you thought you ever could, and you'll have more muscles that ache than you ever knew you had. And you may not even get to wrestle in competitions." I just said let's strap on the headgear and get rolling. It was like all I could see. I didn't care any about what he said. I'd just caught the bug to wrestle and nothing was going to get in my way. I told my coach that and he just smiled and said, "Come on aboard, son. That's the attitude you need."

Kelvin, age 17

4. *You can develop excellence.*

When you are enthusiastically committed to your vision, you make it possible for your gifts to stand out and for you to excel. It often is this commitment to excellence that distinguishes those who are truly committed from those who want something but aren't willing to put forth the effort to achieve it.

A friend told me recently about finding commitment to excellence in a most unusual place—a state driver's license examining station in a strip shopping mall in Peoria. This examining station employed a fellow named Earl Dempsey, who had retired from a job as a coffee company salesman and started a new career as the photographer for driver's license photographs. After seventeen years in that job, and at the age of seventy-eight, Dempsey was still so committed and enthusiastic that people from all over Illinois drove to *his* station to have their driver's license photographs taken, according to a newspaper story about him.

The story noted that taking driver's license exams and having your photograph taken is considered an unpleasant and irritating requirement of government—except at Dempsey's station. His good humor, gentlemanly manner, nonstop chatter, and really bad jokes affected everyone there. People actually *smiled* in their driver's license photos taken by him, because by the time they'd filled out all the forms and taken the tests they'd become infected with his enthusiasm.

> When you are enthusiastically committed to your vision, you make it possible for your gifts to stand out and for you to excel.

My brother laughed at me when I told him I got a part-time job at McDonald's. He wanted to know if Ronald McDonald himself had interviewed me. And you know, I saw plenty of employees who did the bare minimum, but no more. I just figured, what the heck, if I'm going to work here, I might as well have fun while I'm doing it. And it's fun when I throw myself whole-heartedly into something. So that's what I did.

Aaron, age 16

5. *You can inspire others to help you.*

The enthusiasm and passion you bring to a commitment inspire excellence. Excellence in turn inspires others to care about your commitment. Think of a teacher or coach or mentor who has played an important role in your life. What makes this person different from other people you came into contact with growing up? Caring and commitment. The teachers who care about their students and bring enthusiasm and excellence into the classroom inspire the same caring and excellence in their students. Coaches who demand excellence inspire it in their players. When you bring passion to your commitment, you inspire others to share your vision and to look for ways to help you. Your enthusiasm is the match that lights the fire of commitment in you and in those around you.

We had a fund-raising goal of $10,000. I remember our first committee meeting; half the committee was saying no way could we raise $10,000. I told them there was no way we *couldn't* raise $10,000 if we really wanted to. I said I knew not only that we *could* do it, but that we *would* do it, that that goal was guaranteed if we all put forth the effort. It just depended on whether we wanted to do it or not. I could see their attitudes changing right then. They went from laughing and being cynical to believing what I said. And we got down to business and raised more than $13,000.

Laurie, age 18

Making Commitments Part of Your Everyday Life

In your commitment to pursue a fulfilling life, three types of commitments are essential. Make these commitments part of your everyday life; weave them into your thoughts and actions. The commitments are

- Celebrating your successes,
- Helping others pursue a better life, and
- Continuous learning and growing.

TEENS CAN MAKE IT HAPPEN

Celebrating success. At first glance, you may think this sounds silly. Who wouldn't celebrate success when it comes? The truth is, however, that people often are not prepared for success. Sometimes they feel undeserving of success, unworthy of it, and they can't handle it. They self-destruct.

Realize this and know that it is good to celebrate your successes. I know that may seem like the least of your problems early in the Success Process, but as I have said throughout this book, to get where you want to go in life, you must become who you need to be. If you don't feel as though you deserve to win a starting position on your team, be cast for a role in the play, earn a high grade in a difficult class, or go to the college of your choice, chances are you won't accomplish those goals.

Commit to success by earning it and knowing that you deserve it. Prepare yourself so that when success comes, you are comfortable with it. Learn to celebrate your successes and acknowledge your defeats, and then move on to the next opportunity and challenge. Celebrating success doesn't mean you coast or put your drive into neutral; it simply means you acknowledge your effort and your accomplishment, and you take joy and pride in it. Note, too, that pride doesn't mean you thump your chest and crow about your achievements; it means you value your gifts and your accomplishments. You appreciate them for what they are. Celebrating success is a healthy way of life.

Helping others. Along with committing to your own success, I'd advise you to also commit to helping others find success, particularly those who are struggling to find their own way. Throughout this book, I have advised you to consider not only your personal development and relationships and your job or career but also your role in the community as you pursue a better life. You don't have to wait until you are on top to do it. My mother, Mary Graham, founded a support group for families dealing with mental retardation and over the years has won many community service awards. Fifteen years ago, I followed her lead when I founded the nonprofit Athletes Against Drugs as part of my commitment to the community.

I did it because I'd grown angry at seeing so many reports in the media about athletes who were using drugs and destroying their lives. So many young men and women appear to be overwhelmed by poverty, low self-esteem, broken families, and a lack of structure in their lives. They turn to gangs, guns, violence, substance abuse, and other antisocial and self-destructive outlets for their feelings of anger and powerlessness. So many young people look to athletes and sports as the only positive outlet for their energies and attentions; I wanted to show them a way out by offering positive role models.

235

The first guy I signed up was a young basketball player on the Chicago Bulls named Michael Jordan. Michael was not difficult to recruit for Athletes Against Drugs. I simply wrote down my concept on a piece of paper and asked him if he would be willing to support it. He signed right up. Athletes Against Drugs now has more than 150 members, ranging from Olympic athletes to top professional golf and tennis players, and professional football, basketball, and baseball stars. The athletes participate in programs for schools and youth organizations so youngsters can have positive alternatives to drugs, crime, and gang membership.

Bob Shannon, the former head high school football coach in East St. Louis, Illinois, offers another example of the value of committing your life to the success of others. What was it about Shannon's career at East St. Louis High School that made him so respected that sports reporters praised him and a book, *The Right Kind of Heroes*, was written about him? After all, he was nothing more than a football coach at a high school in a town so poor that its city hall was once sold off because the town didn't have enough money to pay off a judgment against it in a lawsuit. East St. Louis High School was itself so poor that the showers didn't work, the lockers lacked doors, and the playing equipment was so shoddy it was sometimes difficult to tell who was dressed to play and who was just hanging on the sidelines. Without the money to paint markings on the football field, Shannon had to burn the yardage markers and sidelines into the grass with weed killer that he paid for himself.

Shannon, who was once named the national coach of the year, rose above an impoverished background himself, but that is not what made him so respected. Nor is it the fact that his coaching record over nineteen seasons in East St. Louis was 193–33, with six state titles and sixteen playoff appearances.

The heroic aspect of Coach Shannon's life lies not so much in what he did for himself; it lies more in what he did for the young people around him. He helped hundreds of young athletes pursue better lives by motivating them to get into college. He demanded of his players, most of whom came from impoverished families, that they make a *commitment* not only to their teammates and to winning, but also to bettering their lives.

"I am about commitment," he has said.

For Shannon, it wasn't how good you are as an athlete; what mattered to him was what kind of person you wanted to become. On Shannon's teams, players were cut from the team for lack of commitment. He once kicked a star quarterback off the team because the player refused to take off his earring. Leaders didn't wear earrings in Shannon's book. They committed fully, or they didn't play.

By sharing his commitment and demanding the same from his players, Coach Shannon enriched the lives of hundreds of young people and made his community, and his world, a far better place.

You don't have to be a coach or a teacher or a doctor or a lawyer or a business owner to help someone. Look around you. You can help people right now. You can help by offering encouragement and support. You can be there for friends. You can join a mentoring program for grade school kids. You can make a pact with a friend and hold him or her accountable to goals. You can join in community projects and activities, raising money for causes that you believe in. You can tutor someone in a favorite subject area. You can volunteer for student committees or for nonprofit organizations or for hospitals or nursing homes within your community. You have plenty to offer to the people around you—your friends, your peers, your community—right now.

Learning and growing continuously. If you want to be successful and maintain success, you have to commit to a lifetime of learning and growing. Learning refers not only to formal education, but to self-education: reading; traveling; exploring new fields and new training; and continual personal, spiritual, and intellectual learning. The U.S. Department of Education reports that most adults will have at least three significant job changes in their lifetime. That means you will need to keep your mind sharp by continually developing your ability to absorb new information while building your emotional and spiritual strength to handle all that life throws at you.

How do you do this? By seeking knowledge. A study on reading habits by the publishing industry recently found that the laziest readers are young adults under the age of twenty-five. People in this category purchase only 4 percent of all books sold. Now, the study noted that it may be that this age group buys fewer books because it has less disposable income than others. I hope so. As someone who did not become an avid reader until relatively late in life, I realize the importance and value of lifelong learning through reading.

Reading as much as you can find about your areas of interest will open up your world for you. You might not get to where you want to be in your life if you don't make the effort to find out how to get there by reading and learning.

When you keep up with the issues and interests that are important to you, you are also committing to bettering your life. The great Frederick Douglass recognized this fact when he said, "When you are working with your hands, they grow larger. The same is true for your heads. Seek to acquire knowledge as well as property."

Know that when you commit to your vision, you must also commit to *continuous* growth. Stephen Covey refers to this

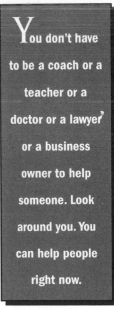

You don't have to be a coach or a teacher or a doctor or a lawyer or a business owner to help someone. Look around you. You can help people right now.

never-ending striving to better your life and the world around you as the *upward spiral*. I have heard others describe it as *living peak to peak*. Both are descriptions of a continual cycle of growth in which every goal you attain becomes a springboard to a higher level of achievement.

You grow by constantly renewing your commitment to bettering yourself in all your Success Circles. Why should you strive to grow even after you have achieved a goal? Because that is what makes for a dynamic and rewarding life. Why sit life out if you can challenge yourself to develop your talents and skills even more? Why not take it all the way to the wall, using up every ounce of energy, every bit of creativity, every resource that the universe provides?

Listen to what your inner voice says. What does it tell you after you've sat around the house all day watching television? *I feel like a lump.* What does it say after you've cleaned the garage, mowed the lawn, cleaned up the yard, written a good paper for a class, or jogged five miles? *I feel energized. I feel like I accomplished something.*

What will your list of accomplishments be at the end of your life? Will it be a long list? Listen to that inner voice and cultivate it. Use the steps in the Success Process as your guidelines for pursuing a better life that forever follows the upward spiral.

■ Committing to Excellence

Success is found through the pursuit of excellence. It is tied in to your relationships with others as well as your personal development. Answer the following questions to help you make a commitment to excellence.

How can you commit to help others pursue a better life? Be as specific as possible, naming a particular person, if you'd like.

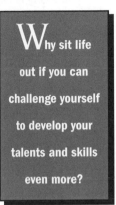

Why sit life out if you can challenge yourself to develop your talents and skills even more?

_____

_____

_____

How will helping others help you in your own pursuit of a better life?

_____

_____

_____

We all need to grow throughout our lives. Name ways you can continue your growth spiritually, intellectually, and emotionally.

Spiritual growth

_____

_____

_____

Intellectual growth

_____

_____

_____

239

Emotional growth

_____

_____

_____

Look around you at the temptations and the distractions of the modern world. Think about how easy it is to give in to those corrupting influences. Why not just kick back and go where life takes you? Why not give in to the seductions of tobacco and alcohol, drugs and crime? Why should you commit to bettering your life?

The answer is simple. If you don't, who will? If you don't pursue your vision of a satisfying life, who is going to pursue it for you? If you choose to settle for less than what is possible for your life, you have no one else to blame for what you get. If you fall into a downward spiral through drugs or crime, will the world cheer you on? Will you fly like Eddie the Eagle? Or will you suffer the consequences of your own laziness and lack of commitment?

Do you want the good life? Take my road. Follow the Success Process, and even the worst days will be better than the best days you'll have in the downward spiral. Why? Because when you follow the Success Process, *you* are in control of your life. You decide where you are going, when you are going, and how you are going to get there. You are in control. A better life is always within your power to achieve.

And when you get to where you want to go, all you have to do is to commit to reaching the next level of accomplishment, and then, once again, you will be on your way, upwardly mobile, to a fulfilling life.

As I stated at the beginning of this book, my goal was to teach you a process for pursuing success and a rewarding life for yourself and for those around you. And as I noted then, I cannot guarantee success or happiness for you, or for myself, for that matter. Each of us can only dream and strive, and in the dreaming and striving, we may well achieve a better life.

Life is only as good as you make it. So make it a good one and enjoy your journey. I'll be cheering and praying for you. Good luck and remember: *You* can make it happen.

Epilogue

The Success Process in Action: A School-Wide Project

You've read the book and you're ready to tackle the nine steps to improving your own life. I want to leave you with the inspiring example of a group of students to whom I am deeply indebted. Thirty-six students from Shorewood High School in Shorewood, Wisconsin, took part in a Leadership Education and Development (LEAD) class that helped me adapt the Nine-Step Plan for Success from my first book, *You Can Make It Happen*, for a teenage audience.

These students, teacher Lisa Bromley, and Shorewood School District director of instruction Linda D'Acquisto helped shape the book you have just read. But that's not all; after mastering the nine steps, the students decided to use the plan to make a difference in their community.

The Shorewood students showed us that the process can work in a larger context—in this case a school-wide project. The Shorewood Games is a student-run, Olympic-style event that had been held twice previously, in 1988 and 1996, but never under the exclusive supervision of students. The students in the LEAD class revived the games and organized a more ambitious event than had been attempted before.

The original inspiration for the Shorewood Games came from Gus Rich, a former Shorewood High student who had spent his high school years fighting leukemia. Students had wanted to show their support for Gus, and the LEAD students wanted to continue the tradition of making a difference.

These generous and confident students involved their entire community in a two-week event that encouraged healthy competition among students, pro-

241

moted school spirit, was lots of fun, and raised money for Midwest Athletes Against Childhood Cancer (MACC Fund). Athletic events were held before and after school and during lunch. Freshman, sophomore, junior, and senior classes competed to earn the most points in volleyball, soccer, basketball, and swimming events. The festivities also included a dance, a pancake breakfast, a tug-of-war, a fun run, and even a fast-food lunch party. Teachers and school administrators pitched in by volunteering for dunk-tank duty and a pie-in-the-face booth. Local businesses donated cash, products and time. The "winning" class got gold medal T-shirts and special honors at the closing ceremony, but the real result was a lot of serious fun, a renewed sense of accomplishment and community for all participants, and a large donation for childhood cancer research.

While everybody agrees that the Shorewood Games were a hit, I think the LEAD students who used the nine steps and created and realized a vision are the biggest winners. This is what the students did:

Step 1: Check Your ID. The twenty LEAD students, all with their own unique confidences, competencies, and capabilities, created an overview of the entire project and then divided into teams that best suited their three *C*s. Some students are great communicators; they worked on publicity, advertising, and announcements. Others are detail oriented; they organized the schedule for the games and handled logistics. A third group was composed of good project managers; they directed complementary fund-raising events, including the fun run, pancake breakfast, and school dance. Each student had abilities that made him or her uniquely able to contribute to the success of the Shorewood Games.

Step 2: Create Your Vision. After they defined their roles, the students needed to create a vision of what they wanted to accomplish. Their vision was big. They wanted a fun and powerful event and they wanted to raise $15,000. To accomplish this they had to set realistically ambitious goals. These questions helped shape their vision

- What are our resources and how can we use them to make the Shorewood Games meaningful and fun? (Take inventory)
- How can we improve on past successes to create the best Shorewood Games ever? (Tap into your imagination)
- What stepping stones will help us get fulfill our vision? (Set goals)
- What members of our community can help us accomplish our goal? (Find guides as you go)

By creating a vision, the students were able to stay focused on achieving a successful Shorewood Games.

Step 3: Develop Your Travel Plan. The Shorewood students pooled their talents and created their vision; now they needed a plan to pull it all together. They identified all they had to accomplish and developed a timeline, budget, and action plan to guide them each step of the way.

Step 4: Master the Rules of the Road. As students began working together to make their vision a reality, they remembered how important it was to establish Rules of the Road. They were stretching themselves and had to take care to maintain their perspective, which meant juggling physical, social, academic, and spiritual concerns.

Step 5: Step into the Outer Limits. The students' bold plan for the Shorewood Games was a challenge that felt risky. By pushing themselves into the outer limits, they found that careful planning limits risk and pays off.

Step 6: Pilot the Seasons of Change. Students learned that while creating and accepting challenge moves them closer to their vision, it creates change in other parts of their lives as well. The experience was empowering and exciting, but the students found it could also be unsettling. For example, many of them felt let down after the prolonged exhilaration of the experience. They learned that such feelings are natural. Understanding the "seasons of change" helped students cope with the emotional ups and downs of this project.

Step 7: Build Your Dream Team. The students learned quickly that to form an effective team—essential to the success of their vision—they had to build mutual trust. As the project progressed, the team jelled and they demonstrated their common commitment to their goal, shared values and expectations, and understanding their complementary roles. They shared a plan for evaluating progress and solving problems and met regularly to monitor progress and to work together to solve unexpected problems.

243

Step 8: Win by a Decision. The students had learned that knowing how to make good decisions is crucial to the Success Process, and they used the five-part process to make important decisions all along the way. For instance, the students determined that they would proceed with the Shorewood Games using the process.

- The weigh-in: From the beginning, the students were clear about their motivation to pursue a special event. They wanted to help sick children, engender a sense of community, and have fun.
- Suiting up: The group explored other fund-raising and charitable options before defining their direction.
- Checking the fit: Among the alternatives, students believed the Shorewood Games would engage the most students and encourage the widest range of participation in the community. As time went by, this judgment was confirmed.
- Stepping into the ring: Once students had committed to the event, they began planning, preparing, and making contacts.
- Go for the knockout: By now the students were committed to their course, and they pursued it with a vigor and dedication that ensured success.

Step 9: Commit to Your Vision. Our students made a commitment to their vision and in so doing exceeded their goals. They never wavered from their plan, and their rewards were great. They drew together their community. They made their schoolmates feel good about themselves by providing opportunities for everyone to contribute and to win. They demonstrated that they are leaders with vision and they made it happen. What else? They raised $20,000 for the MACC Fund, exceeding their own goal by 33 percent!

The LEAD students took a very exciting journey down the road to success and accomplished more than even they had imagined. This story illustrates the amazing power of young people to create vision and make their dreams materialize. You can do the same for yourself or for your school or community, and I hope that you will. Organize your own community event. Mobilize your classmates to support a peer in need. When you use your ability to improve your life, reach your goals, and find success, you can bring others along with you. *You* can make it happen!

Index

245